3 STEPS
TO SILENCE

Re-write the rules and re-train your fearful barking dog

CW01497368

Claire Lawrence
'The Dog Charmer'

Published by WriterMotive
www.writermotive.com

Contents

Introduction

Claire Lawrence 'The Dog Charmer' is a furry dog mum of four, currently living in the Peak District, Derbyshire. After leaving her home in Nottingham with mum and sister at the age of 15, Claire embarked on a journey with her first German Shepherd Dog, Titon.

For the first four years of single dog ownership, it was a dream. Though things soon turned sour when Titon turned into an incredibly problematic pooch. This is where she first faced her own battles with a heavy weight and dangerously out of control barking dog.

This took Claire through hell and high water. Where she was told, it would be better to put Titon to sleep.

Having been to the back and beyond with barking dogs. Claire is now ready and raring to share more of the things she has learned over the years. To help more pet dog owners, just like yourself in bettering managing your barking dog. These are things she teaches daily to her classes, and one to one client's through her business, High Peak Dogs.

Claire finally settled in her dog training career in 2012, and her company has continued to grow ever since. Now being known as the *'The Dog Charmer'* the Peak Districts calmest and most capital barking dog trainer.

Get ready to read more about the experiences for the first time ever. Claire's aim in her training is to bring more calm into the dog owner's lives. Transforming the carnage, she knows first-hand of, that barking dogs can bring. All in just a few simple steps.

Claire's passion for helping chaotic dogs shines through in her two books ' *You'd Be Barking Mad Not To'* and this one in your hands. Soon you will see how she works on more than just the dog. Using a combination of specific touch-based training and silence to benefit you both.

This is a two-way street, and Claire promotes teamwork throughout her teaching, stating: ' *We cannot expect our dog's behaviour to change if we don't first make an effort to change our own.'*

From Perfect to Problematic

What! Surely, I should be telling you the opposite. You want to turn your problematic dog around into a perfect one, correct? Though I don't want to confuse. I do want to tell you about my first experience with a barking dog. one who was as perfect, as perfect could be. By my standards anyway.

The truth is a barking dog can occur at any time of life. So, if you're reading this and have got a quiet dog, excellent to hear but please be aware things could change in this department.

When I was sweet 16, I became the owner of a German Shepherd dog. I had always wanted this breed. The aura of courage, the endless supply of versatile talents. Not to mention them oozing with loyalty and having a breathtaking elegance won me right over.

When he first entered the caravan awning, there were two pups. A male and a female. I had it in my mind, I wanted a bitch. Things didn't work out this way, though. As the breeder came in, holding a puppy under each arm. He placed them on the floor, and this was when it happened.

Soon to be named Titon, he sat and looked around the people in the room, before casually strolling over, plonking himself down right between my feet. He looked up towards me with his soft brown, puppy dog eyes. Intently watching me for a couple of seconds, before shaking his entire little body and slowly lowering himself to lie down.

If dogs could talk, I imagined him to say this: *This cool, yeah?*

As he relaxed at my feet, I glanced up to look at the bitch. Like a coyote after a roadrunner, she was. Busy sniffing and into everything and everywhere, with little interest towards the people around. I think I had a lucky escape there. Though when it boils down it, Titon chose me and I'm eternally grateful he did.

At this time in my life, I had left home and was on the road. There was an argument, and I had decided enough was enough. I was in an *'I'm going'* frame of mind. Most kids would probably return after a couple of hours, realising the error of their ways. Coming grovelling back with an apology and settling down for dinner again. As if nothing had happened

Not me, I'm a stubborn fucker. I left and never returned. Heading for a campsite where I stayed with a friend for a couple of days, before pitching up my tent and contending with the winter months soon to arrive.

I was in and out of places along the way, and after getting Titon, he always with me. Thinking back, it was a bloody stupid idea getting a dog. I mean, I could hardly fend for myself, never mind bringing up and caring for a puppy too. It's amazing what you can do when you set your mind to something though.

For the first four years of single dog ownership, it was a like a ' *Wowing'* magical experience and a Walt Disney's dream. He exceeded my expectations of what having a puppy was like.

In the first few days, owning a puppy is enchanting. You watch them sleep. Oohing and Ahh-ing over how adorable they are. You laugh and smile at their investigative attempts at everything surrounding them. There is no better feeling than exposing your puppy to the world. Where their presence is met with more heart melting moments when other people meet them.

Nope, Titon was never a minute's bother, and he rarely put a foot wrong. It was also an enjoyable experience for me, to see him practically glued to my side where ever I went.

We went everywhere together. And I mean everywhere. As we grew up, Titon maintained his stick to my side character, walking for miles over open fields, down the footpaths and tracks, passing any distractions, you can possibly think of.

Which has just reminded me of a time the breeder came to see me with his dog. Asking if he could take Titon for a walk. I agreed and allowed him to head off with my dog. I watched as all three of them wandered over the field towards a steep man-made track leading up to the disused train track.

There seemed to be no issues, and off they went. Titon racing up the steep incline pulling the guy up with him, and Titon's dad waiting patiently at the top for them.

I returned to doing whatever it was I was doing. Within 10 minutes, I look up to see them all returning across the field. Short, bloody walk, I thought. He may as well have had a coffee here and just threw a ball around for them.

Ha. It wasn't the breeder who cut the walk short. It was the main man himself. At hypersonic speed, Titon came running across the field back towards where I was. Delightfully engaging in bouncing all over me, as if I had been away for months on end.

'He certainly knows how to get his own way! We reached the top, he realised you weren't with us, and that was it. He wanted out.'

Content in my company, Titon wouldn't acknowledge anything we came across. Happily, and politely greeting dogs who came towards him, people and children he wasn't arsed about. Traffic… What traffic? Sheep, Cows, Pink elephants flying on Aladdin's carpet. You name it. He was not bothered.

I remember joking about him not having a voice box because I rarely heard any noises from him at all. Although he wasn't a fan of people trying to hug me. A warning growl came out when this happened.

So, Where Did It All Go Wrong?

After one of the adventures, we were returning to the farm on which I had upgraded myself to a caravan situated within the Peak District, Derbyshire. I had moved away from the hustle and bustle of Nottingham and found a campsite, which was a complete dive, to be honest.

I was sure the family who owned it were all interbred. Speaking in a thick set Derbyshire accent and there just weren't all there at all. I swear I saw six fingers, ten toes and a couple of bolts through the neck. Yep, they were rough. The place was rough. But the rent was cheap, and it was a better option than the tent I had grown to hate.

Back then, I was in less than the conventional type of relationship. Although my life had improved in terms of accommodation and a safer place to sleep in the winter months. Things weren't as they should have been. The only healthy thing in my life back then was Titon.

After two hours of exploring with ma boy, we were walking back down the yard, towards the farm. Ahead of me, I could see an off-lead dog, which I didn't really think much about. I glanced down at the now almost 60kg hunk of black and tan fluff, walking calmly by my side.

I turned my attention back to where the off-lead dog was roaming, I then saw two more dogs appear from behind one of the caravans. I couldn't see an owner. One of the farm gates into the campsite was directly situated behind the 'Clampett's' house. This was the nickname everyone gave to them.

In the English dictionary, a Clampett is described as a hill billy or a scruffy uneducated person. It's usually quite a derogatory description of someone but trust me when I tell you these were the exact definition of one. The insult is said to have derived from the rags to riches story of the Beverly Hillbillies, who brought the unsophisticated but much-loved Clampett family to American TV screens back in the 60s and early 70s.

Anyway, as we passed through the farm gate, I noticed Titon's expression change. I wasn't clued up on canine body language back then, but I still had a strong gut feeling. The type you get when you know something is wrong.

Whenever we feel conflicted about someone or something, we hear the same thing over and over: <u>Trust your gut instinct.</u>

Your instincts help you to navigate through the world easier. This happens by creating mental shortcuts, which help us act quickly. Instead of using energy to fully assess a situation, our brains look for fast answers.

But just how true are your gut feelings?

13

From the way Titon had rearranged himself and with what happened next. Mine was on point. I was always very trusting of Titon's instincts, especially. He had never let me down, in telling me *this* person wasn't to be trusted. Credit due to the lad too, because he always turned out to be correct.

Due to the sheer size of him, I regularly experienced the look of worry on societies faces. It wasn't uncommon for us to have many a dirty look in our direction, and I lost count of the number of times, people disapproved of me owning such a large breed of dog.

Some going to the extent of telling me this. I had the confidence then he was a much better- behaved dog than most others. It boiled down to people fearing his size, which I could see and understand further down the line.

On most occasions and being the confident and sarcastic individual, I once was, these remarks and insults towards my dog were not met with understanding. My favourite response was always one to quieten the narrow minds and shock them into thinking twice about what they said next.

'It's not the dog you have to worry about' A little fucker I was.

He was the BFG of the dog world. A gentle giant who bothered with nothing. Always opting to stay by my side. Although the hugging thing did start to be a cause for concern. He became less tolerant of these before it all happened.

Let's get back to the farm dogs. I took my eyes of Tidge, turned myself after closing the gate, and saw all three of these dogs charging towards us. Full speed ahead, like a plane bolting down the runway, ready for taking off. I didn't know what to expect, but I knew it wasn't gonna be good.

The dog leading the charge was like a collie cross. Black, white and tan, of medium size and he, had this scruffy looking fluffy patch on the top of his head. I had seen the dog around before but never encountered him while I was walking with big T.

Closer they came, and I could see the pearly white teeth begin to appear. Even I knew now, this dog was coming for a fight.

Titon had never been involved in a fight before. Heck, he'd never even experienced this type of confrontation with another dog. He was as placid as could be. How would he cope? What would he do? Were they going to massacre him?

To name but a few thoughts, racing through my mind.

In times of the previous confrontation from other dogs, such as a growl or a dog being unsure of the meet. Titon would simply turn and walk away. There wasn't an option for this, today though.

I had tried to re-open the gate to get back through, but I wouldn't have done it in time. The dogs were virtually on top of us.

Launching himself into the air, only a few feet away now, the collie made his move. Titon intercepted the flying dog, and they began to fight. It was all happening so quickly. I must say, I was somewhat amazed at his skill set in keeping the collie at bay.

Shortly after, the other two dogs arrived at the scene and activated their input into the brawl. All be it with a third of the intent, the collie was conveying. I watched in disbelief as Titon kept all three of the dogs at bay. Not even one of them could touch and keep hold of him.

Walking on all fours, brown bears have an approximate height of 3.5 feet, (just over 1 metre) and they can reach heights of 6-7 feet when standing on their hind legs. I am roughly 5ft 5. Titon exceeded my height level when he placed his paws upon my shoulders for a hug. He loved a good hug, did the Tidge.

If you've ever watched David Attenborough's programs, then a bear fighting is precisely how I can explain this scenario to you.

I continued to watch on in amazement as his head twisted and turned with incredible precision, fending off each one the dogs. Putting them to the floor, before returning to strike the next opponent in the contest.

The time came, where the other two dogs became hesitant of returning for another attack. I can't blame them. Titon really was making mincemeat of their attempts. Considering his size, he was quick, agile, and precise. The departure of the two four-legged bystanders, now meant Titon could focus specifically on the collie.

His jaws impounded and encompassed the neck region. I imagined the force of each of his bites would be like a sled hammer with teeth. Resulting in some severe damage if he had wanted to.

Thankfully and preferably, he opted to only hold the collie dog in place on the floor. Occasionally there was a wriggle and more of an attempt to free himself from the chops.

This was pointless. Titon would give a mini-shake, letting out a growl and holding the position, a little firmer.

In total, this fight was probably only a few minutes long. I can tell you now, it felt like an eternity. Logical thoughts entered my brain, and I realised sooner or later, I was going to have to do something about this. What could I do? What should I do?

I was hesitant at putting my hands in to split them up.

From the way, things were going. Titon was doing a pretty good job of sorting it out himself. His weight and positioning in this fight were his most valuable tool. This dog wasn't getting out of the hold, Titon had on him. Rather like how a wrestler encircles his opponent's head with one arm.

Eventually, there was what seemed like a window of opportunity to split the dogs up. The owner had now appeared, understandably worrying to high heaven. And the other dogs removed from the scene.

My concerns were heightened every second Titon had a hold of the neck. What would he do next? I had never seen him behave in this manner before. I wasn't even aware of his capabilities in a situation like this.

Then the thought came to my mind, and an alarming feeling of dread and despair took over me. *What if he bites down harder? What if he kills this dog...?*

With an over-reactive owner, me now in a heightened state of shock at my dog's behaviour, what I witnessed next, panicked me even more.

'I wouldn't do that!' I called out.' But it was too late.

I Started Getting Used To The Bad, But Then It Got Worse

Knowing what I know now, Titon had viewed this man as another attack. At the time, my feelings of shock, concern, responsibilities closely followed by doubt on his fighting intentions, greatly intensified. I now had an even bigger problem to contend with.

There are many advantages to being young. One of the main things you have is an endless supply of energy along-side a limited amount of responsibilities. Perhaps you had a job and a car to pay for but had little worries in doing so because you had a roof over your head and your hot meals cooked for you every evening.

And if things got tight with your money because you spent the last of your wages on extra shots at the local club, you could simply call on a cash advance from your parents to help you out.

You can afford to make mistakes. It's the way we learn. It's easy to pick yourself back up, dust yourself off and move on from the errors we encounter as youngsters. Then learning from it and avoiding those mistakes when the situation arises again.

There wasn't any calling on my parents in this situation though. Departing from home at such a young age meant I was now facing this alone. By the second, my primary responsibility was turning sour. And I couldn't think of anything logical and safe to do about it.

While attempting to find the collar to hold and split up the dogs, Titon had spun his head around and snapped at the collie's owner. We soon found out how severe this snap had been.

Dogs do something called re-direction. Basically, they are so in the moment of fighting or emotional state, they lash out at anything and everything around them. Some call it the red zone, I call it as 'he viewed the contact, as another attack'

By performing this snap and redirecting on to the man, Titon had caught his left wedding ring finger and taken the limb clean off, right down to the second knuckle.

'Shit'

I don't think anyone had fully comprehended what had just happened until the man held his hand up in the air towards his face, where we all saw the remnants of the missing finger.

There are approximately 90 muscles in the human face used to show somebodies emotions. I couldn't tell you precisely how this guy's face looked but what I can say for sure is how his face turned a ghostly shade of white, and the bug-eyed look of horror appeared as he processed what he saw in front of his face.

He lowered, then held his injured hand with the other just in front of his chest. Watching on as the blood continued to pour down his arms, from the wound. He attempted to mutter out some words, but it had already tipped him over the edge. His attempt to speak failed him, and before I knew it, he had fainted and fallen to the floor.

By this time, there was a small congregation of people around where the fight was happening. The Clampett's were there but were neither use nor ornament, so a couple of people with brains in their head went to assist the man.

I felt like I was at the door to hell. I watched on as they helped the guy, before turning towards the remaining people watching the dog fight and looking at me with disgust and concern. There was no way anyone else was going to help me with these dogs after what had just happened.

A continuous statement ran through my mind. '*What the hell do I do?*'

I knew this was on my shoulders, I had to at least try to break up this ordeal. After seeing what I 110% believed to be my perfect and problem-free pooch, do something so severe and out of character, I had no idea how Titon would respond next.

I vaguely remember hearing one of the farmers saying '*T here's only one sure fire way to stop all of this nonsense. I'll go and get my shotgun before someone else gets hurt.*'

To fuck with you, I thought. There was no way on this god damn earth I was going to watch my dog get shot for something that wasn't initially his fault. On went the big girl panties and over I went.

To say I had a good relationship and bond with Titon was an understatement. We were so close, and I always told myself he would never harm or let any harm come to me from anyone. I was confident I could walk anywhere and everywhere with him, at any time of the day. With him by my side, I was always safe.

Claire Lawrence

Though witnessing what I had just seen bought over a seriously black cloud of hesitation and doubt on what I knew I needed to do.

The importance of having a good relationship with your barking dog will become more apparent as we go through the book. It really is an essential element to have, especially with a fearful dog. This bond turned out to be the saving grace for me on this day. I went in.

As I began to approach, I slowly assessed the whole situation and contemplated the best course of action to take. I watched on as Titon was holding the dog firmly in place by the neck. His eyes fixed like a sniper, laser-focused on the target and ready to fire. I eyeballed at the dog on the floor and could see he was struggling to breathe. Yet for some unknown reason, I remained completely calm.

Calm or struck down with intense fear, I'm not 100 percent sure. But I wasn't panicking in a flutter or screaming like a wimpy girl who'd just seen a spider... Ahem, more on this later.

I inhaled and exhaled deep breaths, putting one foot in front of the other until I was yards away from the jaws of my dog. One thing you will learn from my teaching is how remaining calm is a vital component to master with barking dogs. On this occasion, it wasn't intentional, but over the years the calmer I have stayed, the better the outcome has been. The first lesson of the book for you.

I hesitantly knelt in the square patch of grass on the campsite we were in, popping back up in reflex reactions when I thought a strike my way was coming.

'Okay pal, that'll do now.'

I uttered these words with no idea what-so-ever as to how they would be met. I was close enough for Titon to hear me, yet not too close in case he lashed out and turned on to me. I watched as his eyes slowly moved to the side where I was positioned.

If you've never noticed the wind currents flowing through the woodlands and trees, it is naturally soothing. Like a song towards those who pay attention to and hear it. Titon's intake of breath resembled this powerful passion the gusts have, as they rearrange the autumn fallen leaves and summer seeds being blown around settling in their place to plant and grow.

As he exhaled with a huff of sheer power, I nodded at him before moving a little closer. His eyes were locked on mine, and I mimicked his breathing. I lifted my left hand before making an advance towards him and slipping my fingers underneath his collar.

'Come on now, that'll do pal. Release. Good boy'

Almost instantly my words had an immediate effect, and he let go. This is called trust.

Unfortunately, although my requests and words of reassurance had released his jaws from the other dog's neck, it didn't stop the collie dog coming back for another pop at him. Before I had a chance to block a second scrap, the two were fighting once again.

When the opportunity came around again, I repeated the same process which had worked before. This time and understandably, Titon was more hesitant in letting go. I continued reassuring him and this time roped in a second pair of hands to take hold of the collie.

Titon clearly trusted me enough to let go again, and the fight was over.

I immediately put him in the back of my car, which was situated a few feet away from where the chaos had been happening. No sooner had I put him the boot of my teeny tiny Citroen AX car, I looked up to see a police car entering the campsite. This was the last thing I wanted, but after explaining what had happened and the injured guy not wanting to press charges, Titon was safe.

This was an incredibly nerve-wracking experience for me. I had never been in any trouble before, and I didn't intend on getting in any. The police man was quite helpful and understanding about the whole thing. Stating how only an idiot would put their hands into a dog fight.

'There's no damage to the other dog, and I'm happy with this just being one of those unfortunate situations. Go and make sure he has no injuries either and grab yourself a brew.'

Have you ever been so relieved about something, you almost wet your knickers with joy? Aye, this was how I felt when I heard these words and watched as the police car departed from the yard. Titon and I headed back into our caravan, and it was all now finally over.

Though it wasn't over for us yet. In fact, this was merely the beginning.

Testimonials

'It's not very often a dog training book comes along which is brutally honest, extremely helpful and a hugely entertaining read, Three Steps to Silence is such a book. Claire has produced a jargon free, simple to follow barking blueprint that takes a stressed out dog owner by the hand, and guides them through the process of understanding why your dog barks so much, then shows you how to re-connect, better manage and rehabilitate your barking dog.

Fear barking is a subject which needs careful handling, but Claire has done a brilliant job of tackling this difficult topic, and she has truly earned her 'Dog Charmer' title. Well done Claire!'

Dominic Hodgson - The King of Canine Common Sense
www.growyourpetbusinessfast.com

'5 Amazing Book! A must buy for anyone having issues with their dogs barking, even if your dog isn't barking out of fear, or if you are not sure – this will help you understand your dog's actions more and in turn help improve your dog's behaviour.*

A great informative and even entertaining real with fabulous analogies in simple terms for pet dog owners. I will be recommending to all my barky dog clients. A must read for anyone who has ever had those judging looks and comments from other when out on walks with your dog'

- Sarah Bartlett, KCAI Hound Helpers LTD.
www.houndhelpers.co.uk

'This book is a must if you have a dog that barks a lot. It can be really hard if your dog continuously barks, trying to understand why. We're often led to believe that they are attention seeking. Claire will show you that it's actually not attention seeking behaviour, and more often than not, its fear based.

Three steps to silence gives you the tools to understand what your dog needs from you to help eliminate the fear that causes their barking. Claire takes you on a journey describing her own troubles with her dogs, past and present, that have had barking issues. As a professional dog walker, I will be recommending this book to my clients who have barking dogs. I will also be using the knowledge I've gained from reading this book in my walks with said barking dogs.'

-Sally Cousins, Woofer Walkies.
www.wooferswalkies.com

'Emotional rollercoaster from start to finish. Claire makes you feel sad, then crying out with laughter. I wish I had read this book when I had my barky Shepherd. I think it would have made all the difference. Claire teaches you the 'Fear Barkers' guide which will help any pet owner. Not only does she help you understand why your dog is barking but also offers practical steps to help you make the situation manageable. I would stress, do not read if you are not willing to the hard work in.'

- Harriet Goodall, Pawtastic Gun Dog Specialist.
www.pawtasticpetsitting.co.uk

'Claire's book is an entertaining and thought provoking read. I have learnt a lot about why dogs bark and where I have reinforced the wrong behaviours with my pair of terriers. Back to school for me and my dogs with the help of Claire's book.'

- Bruce Taylor, with Milly and Paddy

'Love this book! A fantastic read for anyone who has a fearful barky dog. Claire's personal experience with dealing with this problem shines through. She shares her successes as well as her failures with her own dog, so that the reader can learn from her mistakes. Her common-sense approach is easy to understand and implement. Definitely a book I will be recommending to clients that have fearful barky dogs.'

- Natasja Lewis, DipCABT, dog trainer at Nightsabre Dog Training and Behaviour. Author or 'No Pulling Allowed' and 'Dogz Thinkz Differentz'

'3 Steps To Silence lays out the pillars of canine training, learning and communicating. Despite being steeped in fact and logic, the book reads like a lively conversation with a friend. Often, we're so frustrated that we're not even thinking about why our dogs bark, we just want them to stop. 3 steps to silence teaches you how to identify a dog that is barking out of fear and then gives us a three-step plan to help them.

Kind, modern and reward-based, Claire encourages us to see the world from a fearful dog's point of view. She gives us practical tips such as what to do is another dog is heading straight for your fearful dog at break neck speed. The stories Claire tells about her experiences with her own barking dogs are entertaining and often gut-wrenching. Claire has lived it. Put your trust in her.

If you're professional, read it now, recommend it to your customers, give it to rescue dog owners! It is fact packed but light hearted, jargon-free but thorough, short but ambitious Whether you're a first-time dog owner or an experienced trainer, we can all benefit from modern dog training perspectives presented in real-life language.'

- Katie Guastapaglia, Enrichment Specialist at Dogwood Adventure Play
www.dogwoodadventureplay.com/

'To be able to read a book that is written by someone who has not only studied dogs but who has hands on experience with their own and client's dogs, is a breath of fresh air. Claire's explanation offer clarity of not only what to look for, but in how to deal with the situation too. Her stories have made me laugh but have given me a very clear explanation of a fearful barking dog. With Claire's stories in my head and clear direction, I highly recommend this book and Claire at High Peak Dogs.

If you want results, do the work and listen to Claire 'What gets rewarded, gets repeated' Bloody brilliant!'

- Jennifer Beattie
www.jensjunts.co.uk

'In her practice with my one dog (who is fearful of other dogs) and me, all behaviours have improved as we implement Claire's teaching. My second dog, who I thought was pretty perfect, has improved her already

good behaviours such as recall and loose lead walking as a consequence of Claire's teaching of me.

It is a privilege for me and the dogs to work with Claire and I hope her knowledge within her book will allow her to help many more dog owning families.'

- Sue Johnson, with Dotti and Scout.

Who Is The Dog Charmer?

I wasn't born a dog trainer, nor did I ever expect to write a book on the things I know. Yet, here I am sat in the spare room, tapping away on the keyboard in the little village of Tideswell, Derbyshire.

My name is Claire Lawrence. The owner, and operator of High Peak Dogs. I offer a one to one training experience, focusing intently on getting calm and desirable behaviours from the dogs I work with.

I am a firm believer that not all dogs can integrate into group situations. I'm not a fan of free play, group walks or doggy day-cares at all. This is due to me seeing the after-math of dogs who haven't coped within a pack setting and have had their temperaments ruined from just one bad or negative experience.

You have been welcomed into my world by first reading the story of my first dog, Titon. How he went from perfect to problematic in the space of a few days. This took me down a path I never even knew existed. It wasn't easy, and we had some seriously tough times, but we got there. And before he passed at the grand old age of 12, I could once again walk him anywhere and everywhere. Passing distractions without him panicking or wanting to bite anything.

I am going to assume because you are reading this book, you too, are looking for a solution to your barking dog problem. Which I will provide for you in the 'Figure It Out Fast' chapter.

Barking, in my eyes, is a chaotic behaviour and the basis of this book focus' on dogs barking through fear. There are many forms of barking, and it's a little like spaghetti on your dinner plate in terms of complexity. Though I know, some dogs out there need more hands-on and personalised assistance in the form of a behaviourist, I still believe there are plenty of things you can be doing to prevent this problem from getting any worse.

Before we begin, I'd like you to write down this sentence. And if you only take one thing away from this book. I want it to be this.

What gets rewarded, will get repeated. And for your dog to keep barking, means the behaviour **IS** <u>being rewarded in some way.</u>

In real life, I would always refer to a dog by their name or their sex. He or She. However, the stories within this book are mainly based on my male dogs. So, I will be referring to all dogs as a 'he.'

Currently, I have four furry family friends. Skye is my eldest German Shepherd at 8.5 years old. She's never been a bother. She's definitely the soul dog and an oracle of goodness. Skye has been my demonstrations dog since she was old enough to walk. She's helped puppies with socialising correctly, had worked impeccably well for me in training classes and with dogs of varying age.

She teaches my private coaching client dogs how to copy her and behave. She has chilled out in the face of many a barking dog, shrugging off the conflict and remaining calm while they learn what they should be doing instead of the barking. Big love for Skye.

Hunter is also a German Shepherd. He's the baby of the group at 3.5 years old, but he's the biggest of the lot. A big bloody baby I may add. Hunter is a recovering barking dog and has suffered from fear barking. At the time of writing this, we are making excellent progress, and I can walk him around the village. Where we can see other dogs and distractions, and he can cope well and stay quiet.

Then comes my other little oracle of goodness, all be it in a tinier version. Lilly! A miniature Jack Russell who is approaching 4.5 years old. She can bark when she gets over excited and is a little stress head on the lead, but her ability to work as the next demonstration dog as Skye enters retirement is on point. Anything for a tennis ball and is successfully helping other dogs to learn, she isn't a threat.

And finally, my little ginger ninja, problem child, Digger. He didn't have the best start in life, being kept in a stable until 16 weeks old, then incurring several forms of punishment and disregard from a partner I was with at the time. And has successfully hunted and killed prey items. He doesn't hesitate in taking on dog's other dog's too! He has been, is and always will be a dog I will have to manage. I will never be able to truly trust Digger, to not want to hunt, fight, and kill stuff. Though I accept him for what he is and, I work with what we've got.

In the words of Denise Fenzi, you must work with the dog in front of you.

Most of the stories in this book are based around German Shepherds. Barking isn't only designated to this breed of dog. Any dog can bark. Though being the keeper of the GSD, it merely means most of my stories are based around them.

Working with barking dogs has taught me loads. Not only through education, but also in how we are as human beings too. The first thing to do, as hard as it is, is to remain calm. I'll speak more about this later.

Next up is to sympathise with your dog's emotional state. They aren't barking to be a pain in your side. I care very little for fixing obedience training problems when the mindset of a dog isn't right. If your dog isn't emotional balanced and well, the chance of you fixing anything else is slim.

Finally. Buffoonery! You need a good sense of humour with these dogs (and in reading my books) otherwise before you know it, you'll be sat rocking in your armchair pleading to be sent to the nuthouse.

I'm going to do my best to make the reading process and content in here as understandable for you as I can. Though I will confess something to you and warn you now. I have this irritating and automated tendency to speak in a language you may not understand. Have you seen Harry Potter and the deathly hallows?

We learn in this movie how Parseltongue is the language of snakes and how Harry can use it to communicate with them. To an average human who cannot speak the language, it merely sounds like hissing without taking a breath. Ever heard a pissed off snake?

It's a rare skill, has a bad reputation and it's hard not to use when you're suckered into the lingo land. Dog trainers have their own language, and it's one we cannot help but drift off into. From a pet dog owner's perspective, it's annoying and confusing. How are you supposed to practice something you don't understand?

When you spend your days talking to other dog trainers and reading science articles full of behavioural quadrants, counter conditioning, positive punishment, cognitive brain functions, but to name a few. The language becomes engrossed and automated in our nimble, crazy dog people minds.

Therefore, I'm not gonna use those words or aim to confuse you in any way, shape, or form. I want you to learn. I want you to be able to understand and go away from this book, knowing exactly what you've got to do.

Okay, let's talk a little more about who this book is for and what you are going to master.

Is This The Book For You?

Are you worried about your dog walk before you've even left the house?

Is your early warning radar on and in full swing about what is coming around the next corner or towards you? It can feel like you're always on the lookout, preparing for the next explosion of barking, can't it?

Have you tried everything you can possibly think of to stop your dog from barking, but everything you have tried has failed, and you're still left with a ticking time-bomb at the end of your lead?

Oh, how I remember those days.

The stress, frustration, embarrassment, and daily anger I experienced was enough to nearly send me to the nuthouse. I have had years of these emotions and situations while working and walking with barking dogs. Just know, you are not alone in your struggles.

Barking dogs is up there as one of the main problems dog owners, just like yourself are facing daily. Even as a pet professional, I experience situations where I wish the ground would open and swallow me up.

In this book, I wanted to not only share my not knowledgeable but also my knowledgeable and qualified dog trainer stories with you. And really showing you things, which are proven to work. Listen up, though. This ain't gonna be easy, and you are gonna have to pull your socks up and get to it, if you really want to fix things. You and I both know, something worth having in life is never going to be a walk in the park. You will have to work for it.

In this book, you will learn exactly why your dog is using this specific type of barking and come to terms with how they are genuinely feeling. I want to also detail more about how it looks and sounds, and bust those never fading, BS myths about dogs doing things to be top of the pack. You'll also get given three simple and easy to follow steps to help you with your barking dog.

Once you open your mind and take on board what you are about to read, then put it into practice. You will soon have much more success and be on the road to silence.

One thing I wanted to mention is I have a streak of Irish blood running through me. It's got nothing to do with a barking dog, but it means I tend to swear. In this book and in real life.

I am writing this as I would speak, so if you are offended to the odd swear word, then I recommend you close the book and put the fucking thing down.

However, if you're open minded and have a good sense of buffoonery. Do swear at your dogs, like I do from time to time. And are ready to seek the solutions to your problems. Discovering a quieter, calmer and kinder approach in how to effectively train your dog, then we'd better get a shimmy on and dive straight in.

Turn the page and get ready to enter my realms.

If you want to learn even more about how I work and get additional support, then you can head to my website, which is: www.3sts.co.uk

Right my mucker, let's get cracking.

Chapter One: Face Everything And Roar!

You've heard the phrase '*Fuck everything and run*' right? When Stephen King wrote 'Doctor Sleep,' he turned the usual abbreviation of the word FEAR from the alcoholics anonymous phrase ' *Face Everything And Recover*' and turned it into his own, to fit in with his gory, glorious story and epic war between good and evil.

The *'King phrase'* is a more accurate evaluation and demonstration of how most people will act under pressure when they are afraid. I know for a fact, many of us would instead run away from our problems, then turn and face them. But, like the first quote implies, it's impossible to overcome your fear and get better, unless you start to face it.

I wanted to start this book by defining exactly what fear is and how it can affect us. It is by far one, of the most powerful emotions, and it can have a considerable effect and strain on our bodies and mind. As it can for your dog.

Some people can become so overwhelmed by fear, they want to avoid situations that might make them frightened or anxious. This is a natural response to take, but it can be hard to break this cycle when the fear feelings are continually taking over.

In some cases, it can take over your life. Affecting your ability to eat, sleep, concentrate, travel, enjoy life, or even leave the house to go to work or school. This can hold you back from doing things you want or need to do. Most of this happening without you even realising it.

Regardless of the source of fear, it can immobilize too many people and will prevent them from achieving what they desire and are more than capable of.

Fear and doubt exist to keep us safe. It's not inherently bad or good, but rather a tool we can use to make better decisions. There are lots of different things to make us feel afraid. Being afraid of fires, for example, can keep you safe. If you had no fear or recognition of the danger fire can bring, skipping your way into the flames and sitting down on it. Then you'd soon be like Guy Fawkes on Bonfire Night and burnt to a crisp!

On the other hand, those who fear failure can on occasion, force them to try harder and do better, so they won't fail, but it can also stop you doing well if the feeling is too strong and you give up when things go wrong.

What you're afraid of and how you act when you're scared can vary significantly between each person. But by thinking hard and working out exactly what makes you afraid and why can be the first step to sorting out your problems.

I remember when I lived in a block of apartments which had been converted from an old cotton mill. I had one of those full-length wardrobes with the mirrors on, and it was ideally situated on the ground floor. I'm old before my time because stairs really grind on my already dodgy knees.

Anyway, as I arrived home one day, I went to grab a cardigan. I'm shivering just writing this and it ain't from the feelings of being cold. I entered the bedroom which was conveniently situated to the left of the apartment upon entering. Sliding open the wardrobe, I started to scout through my clothing for something suitable. I opted for the jet black and thick set long cardigan; this was sure to warm me up.

I have quite long and thick brown hair which is forever tickling the back of my neck. You'll often see my throwing out a neck twitch, combined with a shoulder hunch and if you do then don't panic. I'm not fading into a fit or anything. On this twitching, the tickling didn't go away which instantly panics me, and I momentarily freeze, while holding my breath, waiting.

After a short wait, I then make my other automated response of scratching the itch and removing the offending dangles of hair. As I went to do this, I also twisted and glanced into the mirror to take a closer look. In my side vision, I saw the one thing I dreaded seeing the most. Honestly, give me a mass murder blood scene over this shit any day of the week.

The biggest, blackest monstrosity of an eight-legged spider was chilling out on my left shoulder. Not giving two hoots about what was happening what-so-ever. If you hadn't guessed by now, I cannot stand spiders. At this time of my life, I was the one who panicked and fluttered in a screaming frenzy. Proper wimp mode.

Have you ever seen the film *'Street Dance: The Moves?'* This was a family made film back in 2010 where a hip-hop crew and a group of ballet dancers were forced to share the same practice space and had to work together. The street dancers had spectacular moves, some of which I wouldn't attempt to try in my day to day life.

Honestly, if there were recordings available of me panicking at 'the cardigan spider convention,' I would have passed the rehearsals with flying colours. Everything happened so quickly. I remember frantically removing the cardigan, bouncing around the room as I went before launching it onto the bed and leaving the room.

I boing-ed and hopped my way off to the kitchen, shuddering and shaking my whole body and hands in disgust at what had just happened. I created my own sequence of the 'Nutcrackers Arachnophobia Dance' … coming to a screen near you soon.

Fellow spider dancers will likely relate, I'm sure (and I hope) I'm not the only one to have done this. Titon was with me on this occasion, and I'm not sure whether he was in shock too at the whole performance or thought I was crazy, but the lad always went to the source of where I was screaming. He was my chief spider catcher and a fantastic one too.

It was never intentionally taught. As a guarding breed and seeing me in such a tizzy, he used to find the spider. And if in a good position, would drop his big dock off paw directly onto it, flick it around a bit, before rolling over onto his back and repeating a back shuffle several times, making sure it was squished. Then he'd eat it '*BLEURGH!*' He did the same with wasps too.

In the kitchen, I was pretty much hyperventilating, and all rational thoughts had vanished from my brain. I was in full FEAR mode. I fucked everything off and ran. After standing in the kitchen for a good few minutes trying to compose myself, my breathing began to return to normal, and then my thinking, rational, and logical brain came back into play.

'Great, now I have to go back in there and find and remove the damn thing'

Unless Titon got to it first. There was no way on this earth, I would have settled or gone to sleep in the room again if I couldn't find it.

As it stands, I did find the spider. It was underneath my cardigan on the bed, sprawled out just like it was dead. Or so I thought. I went to collect a glass from the kitchen to scoop it up and throw it outside. To come back and find it had vanished. It played dead on me!

I didn't sleep in the bedroom for about a week, and I was on constant high alert until I moved out of the place a month later. Yep, I moved to a new house because of a massive spider who outwitted me. Okay, slight exaggeration, I had planned to move out anyway, but this incident was another tick on the go, go, go button.

What Causes Fear?

During the early beginnings of life, nature developed the amygdalae as a specialised purpose organ in the brain, to remember and respond to danger signals. They become sensitive to sensory cues, which accompanied past painful events.

Such sensitivity in the amygdalae of animals has been extensively confirmed. In typical experiments, rats were exposed to painful foot shocks, which was accompanied by a sound. Later, when the noise alone was heard, its amygdalae fired off the fear signals.

As essential as any other part of our brain, the amygdala is the primary defence response mechanism. It recognises danger patterns and impels us (and our dogs) to fight, freeze, or escape.

Fear is determined by the level of imminent danger. Worry and anxiety are triggered by the anticipation of being harmed in the future. Dread, terror, and panic concern the immediate present. At the highest levels, terror and panic can easily overwhelm people, causing them to make irrational choices.

If something terrible has happened to you in the past, then you are going to be fully aware of a similar situation again in the future. There's no telling exactly what causes fear in each individual.

I've had some pretty shit things happen to me over my time so far, and it was suggested to me I shared these with you to some degree, in this book. At first, I completely resisted, because it filled me with dread and yep, you guessed it. Fear.

So, although I'm not going to share the details with you, just know when you've experienced stressful or traumatic situations, it does affect you in some way.

Though I'm often told with my poker face and bubbly personality, you'd barely know anything was wrong at all. I'm mentally strong, and these days, I can quickly turn my negative and fearful outlook on things, into positives. This is merely down to practice.

A favourite phrase of mine is this:

'We cannot expect our dog's behaviour to change unless we first start to change our own.'

Now, I'm not really one for TV, but there are a couple of things I will always sit down to watch. I know... how random a conversation change was this eh but stick with me.

David Attenborough takes prime place, and I am more than happy to watch episodes I have seen before, repeatedly. As I am for the series Friends and MasterChef.

There is one program though, I am completely fascinated with it because it focuses specifically on facing your fears. Ant Middleton and other ex-Special Forces soldiers recreate the SAS's secret selection process and put the recruits through it. Testing them to the ultimate and intense extremes of their physical and more importantly, psychological resilience.

The TV show pits contestants against harsh environments all around the world. The last one I watched at the time of writing this book was set in the mountains of Morocco. This training course is known worldwide as being a notoriously challenging program and has been known to claim the lives of those who take it on.

I watched on in amazement and seen them being put to physical exhaustion for hours on end. Carrying rocks and burdens above their heads and I was in somewhat of a shock but intrigued state when they were doing the interrogation test for 24 hours. Placed and held in stress positions.

Being played distressing sounds such as babies crying for hours on end, to see if they could break them. It nearly broke me with the noise of child screaming over 30 seconds, never mind 24 hours

Whatever you may fear in your life, I am going to presume your dog's behaviour is one of them. I say this because I too worry about how my dogs are going to respond to things. Yeah, I have those same thoughts and feelings with my barking dogs, as you do with your own.

I'll talk more about my gang as we go through the book, but now I've explained a little more about what fear is from a human perspective, let's look at things from your dog's angle because you'll soon find it isn't too dissimilar.

The Dog's Perspective

Fear.

It sounds so simple, doesn't it?

We both know what fear feels like, and your dog isn't any different. The simplicity of the statement is easy enough to comprehend, but the diagnosis and actions from a fearful barking dog aren't so easy to catch on to.

I imagine you envision the look of fear in your dog, differently to how I do. Fear in the English Dictionary is described as follows:

'An unpleasant emotion caused by the threat of danger, pain, or harm' OR ' to be afraid of someone or something, as likely to be dangerous, painful, or harmful'

This part, I feel people understand well enough. The problem with fear-based barking is to the human eye, the behaviour being presented often looks more aggressive than it does scared. Leaving it hard for people to comprehend how their dog is really feeling.

There are two types of fear in the dog world.

Fear submission: This is the one most people can spot and relate too. It's obvious when a dog is cowering and looking worried, they're scared, right?

Submission motivates a dog to react to a threat by attempting to solve the situation by surrendering.

Though this isn't a book on Fear Submission. The behaviour I am discussing here with you today comes in another form.

Fear Defensive . This is the one people often struggle to comprehend. A dog can get so scared, they try to fend off the problem themselves. And what is the only thing a dog has and can use to properly defend themselves?

That's right, it's their mouth. Be it a growl, bark, snap, or the use of their pearly white teefs as a bite.

This defensive type of barking is more common than you may first realise.

An incorrect diagnosis of why a dog may be barking is a significant factor for people dismissing and jumping to the wrong conclusions on what is really happening.

But it isn't just incorrect knowledge here. Many other factors can lead to a dog becoming scared and feeling the need to protect themselves.

And I say protect themselves because this is what they are doing. They are not protecting you, which is what most people are led to believe.

The things I hear from dog owners as to why their dog is barking are almost, always wrong. That's not me blowing smoke up my own arse on how much I know either. This is me trying to teach you what you think you know about dogs and why they bark, isn't always correct.

Spotting fear amongst those barking episodes in your dog can be hard for you to comprehend. I know because it was for me when I first started learning about it.

'He's not scared, he's acting like a maniac killer dog. How can he possibly be scared?'

But the truth is my friend, dogs do bark when they are scared.

When you start to learn why your dog is barking and see things from their perspective, it isn't long before your own emotions and actions begin to change for the better. You start to help your dog more, instead of doing the easy human thing and just telling them off.

You begin to think more before you speak. Work with them more effectively. And you soon start to resolve the problem by following a few simple steps.

Wouldn't it be lovely if our dogs could talk to us and tell us what's wrong? It would be so much simpler to fix. Though what if I told you, your dog is already trying to tell you this?

Dogs are communicating with us all the time. Though they don't speak English, so we need to wise up a little and learn to talk back to them in a language they understand.

It's entirely reasonable for dogs to bark, by the way. It's one way they communicate as a species. This can soon get out of control and become excessive, to the point where they become an utter handful and a nightmare to walk.

After the fight with Titon, this was only the beginning of the reactive road for us. Over the coming days, I started to notice Titon's behaviour changing. The first time it happened, I was totally taken aback and unprepared, to say the least.

I didn't think much about the risks in behaviour changes at the time. He incurred no physical injuries after the fight, he was eating and drinking fine, toileting wasn't a problem either. Other than him glancing around at me while pooping with a look of disgust on his face, as I examined the outlet to see if I could see any signs of the missing finger passing through.

What I thought I'd do with the limb if I did find it, I'll never know. I'm sure nobody in their right mind would want their finger back after a German Shepherd had shit it out their arse.

So, I did what any average person would do and carried on the way we were before. We returned to our long walking adventures, but things just weren't the same.

He started to venture further away from me. He wasn't listening to me like he used too. And god help me when I say this, but he was guilty of jumping a dry-stone wall and chasing off after a flock of sheep one day. He got hold of one too. I was insanely mortified when I realised what was happening.

The day came where my concerns went from '*oh bloody hell Titon*' to ' *Oh My God, I'm so sorry, he's never done this before.*'

One day we were coming to the end of a long walk. Must have been knocking on for a couple of hours, when we reached the main road. I popped him back on the lead and went to cross over.

As we got to the other side, we continued with the road-side path, and ahead of us, I saw a couple and their dog approaching to do the same crossing we had just completed.

When they got within talking distance, if the ground could have swallowed me up, I would have been eternally grateful. As the gap closed between us, Titon lunged directly towards the dog, narrowly missing grabbing hold of it. It came out of no-where and for what seemed like no apparent reason.

Naturally, I apologised as I struggled to hold on to the lead and get Titon out of the way. Understandably the response wasn't *'It's okay, don't worry about it'*

Something I used to get with Titon was dirty looks and panicked parents, collecting their children up off the floor when they saw us approaching. Before he turned problematic.

So, when the time came where he was developing a severe barking issue, you can imagine the responses I incurred.

He became painfully difficult and terribly dangerous to even take outside. These comments I received increased. While hanging on, doing nothing but watching him barking and lunging towards another dog. A passer-by called out to me the words I will never forget until I die.

'That's nothing a needle from the vets wouldn't sort out'

It was a statement which hit harder than a punch from Ricky Hatton in the boxing ring. Deep down and in the real sense of where we were at with Titon's behaviour, I knew this was true. A needle really would sort this out. Not an option I had considered of course, not until after hearing it out loud anyway.

My dog had become a danger to society, and I had no clue how to fix it. Maybe I would have to put him to sleep. Titon went some of through the dominance style 'training' methods. Before I knew any better, I did everything wrong with him.

Every which way I turned, people and internet sources were telling me to correct his behaviour, tell him off, do the stupid Cesar Milan *'Chhhh'* thing and kick him in the stomach when he was barking, like riders do with a horse to move them on. All in the name of the dominance crap which still lingers around today like a smelly fart cracked out in the house by your dog.

Dominance in dogs is a topic to fill an entire book by itself, so I'm not going to go into it too much. I may mention it, though it will be aimed heavily on why you don't need to take that approach.

With everything I was doing to try and fix Titon's barking problem, I ended up it ten times worse than it ever needed to be. When you fight fire with fire, guess what? You're gonna get more fucking fire.

You're Only Human, But It's Time To Be More Dog

It's natural to feel negative thoughts towards your dog when they kick off. Before you know it. You start to feel a lot of anger and frustration rising within yourself. Quickly reverting to shouting, telling them off or perhaps yanking or slapping them with the lead.

Let me tell you something. None of this helps, and it certainly won't fix the underlying problem. Not on an emotional level anyway. Always keep in mind your dog is reacting through fear, and it starts to do something to you internally too.

When a dog is fearful, they are expressing emotion, and as we have already spoken about, this emotion is one of concern. They're scared. What good's a telling-off gonna do? The only thing it really does is to make the handler feel better for a moment in thinking they are doing something about the problem.

Yet a few more steps down the road or a couple of silent minutes in the house and the dog barks again. A sense of Deja Vu occurs, and they find themselves repeating the same telling-off process. It's a vicious circle! So, what exactly has the dog learned?

If you must continue telling your dog to be quiet or to do something, then I'm sorry to be the bearer of bad news, but this isn't dog training. It's management. With this, you will always have to continue telling your dog what to do. Wouldn't it be better to get your dog to a point where they just knew what to do automatically?

By starting to think more like your dog, can really be the difference between failure and success. After all, you are a team, and you will be working together once you start to follow my carefully laid out training plan.

When I entered the realms of reward-based training, after all the silly and pointless punishment ways. I began to see a massive difference in a super short time. Once I started viewing the walk as Titon did, only then did I become fully equipped with a better and much more effective strategy to begin solving the issue. Consideration, patience, understanding, and kindness saved our relationship.

Instead of being a twat towards him and taking the 'easy for my feelings' route, I started to predict when he would bark. I already knew the things Titon was going to bark at, so this part was easy. The distance at which he reacted took a little longer to figure out, but we got there through trial and error.

At the end of the day, it's the evening... joke-sees! Me and my sarcastic humour.

At the end of the day, I didn't want to be battling a 60 kg barking dog anymore, not to mention the danger he presented. And I certainly didn't want to be faced with another statement of *'Put him down'* ever again.

I didn't want my dog to be upset and scared, either. As a dog owner, you only ever want your dog to be happy, don't you? When an animal comes into your life, you would (or should) move mountains to ensure they don't get injured or feel frightened.

I look at this way. What if your dog died tomorrow?

Amid the red rage and battles of the bellowing, have you ever stopped and wondered, *'What was the last thing I said to my dog?'*

Digger is my Border Terrorist; I mean terrier and he is the definition of a difficult dog. With this, he has had a lot of *' I'm sorry dude'* and *'here let's have a snuggle'* when he's utterly pissed me off and sent my frustrations through the roof, to the point where I've snapped.

As horrible as it is to have to think about, it's worth keeping in mind there is only really one downside to a dog. And it's that they only live for a certain amount of time. Which isn't very long at all in comparison to the average human lifespan. Therefore, we should be continually ensuring they are happy, and what I mean by this is mentally.

Excessive barking dogs are generally not in a good mental state of mind.

I remember marking this phrase in my head when my first reaction was to bellow at the dog. My emotions became even easier for me to control once I learned why dogs bark. When I found out its things such as fear, frustration, anxiety, uncertainty, and all things we'd never knowingly want our dogs to feel. I felt 110% appalled with myself.

'My dog has been trying to tell me he needs my help for all of this time, and all I've been doing is giving him a roasting.'

Reality check. Human and canine behaviour collide.

If my dogs died tomorrow, of course, I'd be in a complete and utter mess for days and weeks on end. No doubt about that at all. But I'd be able to say I did everything I possibly could to make sure they were happy, comfortable and safe in my care

- I made the extra effort to get up early and out the door by 5am to give them a pleasant walk while nobody else was around.
- I took the time to walk them individually and teach them they needn't worry or be frightened of other things around us.
- I booted the main problem out of my front door when I truly realised, he (who shall not be named) was constantly making my dogs more fearful daily. They were shit scared to even walk through their own house. This was after Titon I may add, it's incredible how cowards work. Ain't no way on this earth Titon would have allowed that nonsense to happen if he was around.

If my dogs died tomorrow, I can say I gave them everything I could possibly give to only ever keep improving their confidence and trust in me as their guardian. Continuing to improve their behaviour. Step by step.

It's bloody hard to control our emotions sometimes. I know how Jekyll and Hyde our dogs can seem sometimes, but I bet if we asked them the same question, we'd receive a similar answer.

It feels like they are doing it to intentionally wind you up. It sounds so determined and aggressive. Every day, time after time this god damn barking continues. But rather than getting angry with your dog, why not try supporting them instead? Cover up the anger with things such as *'Okay, settle down now pal'* or *'It's okay don't worry.'* It'll save you a lot of stress and meither in the long run.

With this new way of thinking and understanding, it became even easier to avoid putting Titon into a situation where he felt upset and scared. Knowing more about preventing the barking from being used made perfect sense to me. Quite simply, if I saw something approaching us, I would move away from it.

Using field gateways or hopping over stiles made the walk much better. I knew this wasn't the solution to fixing the underlying issue, but the avoidance method in the early stages is an essential thing to do for your barking dog.

Here's where it gets interesting. Creating this distance away from 'the scary thing' then allowed me to teach Titon something else to do instead of the barking. I was happy with silence at this stage. This made him feel safer, and I didn't have to do the dog lead gym work out either. Happier Titon = Happy Claire.

You may well be sat there saying it's all well and good doing this when you have the space to do so, and you'd be 100% right. I was fortunate enough to be in a situation where I could avoid these things most of the time. Though I know, it isn't always easy to do because I now live in a village and still have two reactive dogs under recovery.

But I'm still succeeding with it…

Distractions can often seem to appear out of bloody nowhere, can't they? It feels like I'm in the Legend of Zelda, Breath of the Wild video game when I'm out walking. When I see a corner I can't see around, a part of me dies inside a little. The chances of an intrusion increase dramatically.

You must be in the moment with your dog on the walk though, and not faffing around on your phone. Are you taking in what is around you or are you just checking notifications?

Are you allowing your dog to be a dog and stop for a sniff, or are you hurrying them along and adding additional and unnecessary concern in what is currently a calm situation?

And the big one. Are you taking into considerations where and at what time you are walking?

I know you will meet distractions out there. It's inevitable.

But taking a little more time and putting some more thought in to where and at what time you walk is paramount. I don't expect you to get up and out of the front door at 5am like I have and, still do with my own. But you can avoid the busier times though yeah?

How Difficult Is It To Get What You Want, From Your Dog?

The Story of the stray:

Have you ever been abroad and noticed the stray dogs pottering around the streets?

I have, and from the ones I've seen they are usually chilling out and calm. Never have I ever seen them doing anything completely undesirable, unlike dogs I see in the UK. I don't see them lunging on leads, playing rough with other dogs, jumping up excessively or barking, snapping and biting either.

Nope, I've never seen this, and I've done a fair bit of traveling in my time. I think the main factor for this is they do not have much human interaction, and they can express themselves like a dog should do.

They will likely see humans for sure, and don't get me wrong there are some strays out there with severe behavioural problems but not to the same level or degree as a lot of dogs with human handlers in my opinion.

Dogs are a tolerant and amenable species. These stray dogs have outlets for their natural behaviour and energy levels. It would be understandable for you to presume, with no guidance or structure, these dogs should be wild ass hoons. But they aren't. Think about it for a second. They can do whatever they want, whenever they want. Yet they are still better behaved and calmer than the dogs in human hands.

These dogs make choices every single day. With these choices come consequences. A good or bad outcome will then determine how the dog views the situation again in the future. They learn the same as our dogs do, except they aren't being interrupted or meddled with.

Ain't nobody on the side-lines pulling them away from sniffing the patch of grass with dog pee scent on it. Nor is anyone telling them off for grabbing hold of someone's leftover chips or kebab on the street. Dogs don't naturally choose to use conflict or aggression either.

So, why do our dogs use conflicting behaviours more?

When things are put into context, it isn't too difficult to get what you want from your dog. I appreciate this may seem like a challenging concept for you to understand right now. I mean, all you want your dog to do is to stay quiet and do as they're told, right?

A walk that doesn't feel like a workout. A distraction you can pass calmly and quietly. A simple stress and problem-free walk.

You can get this, my friend, but to do so, you have to first learn to speak in a language your dog is going to understand.

'The key question is NOT how do I stop this behaviour problem? Rather, the question IS, what do I want the animal to do instead? … Then teach it!' - S.G. Friedman, P.H.D

Often, dogs don't get heard. Instead, they get ignored, shouted at, and misunderstood. An animal, regardless of species, still have their own thoughts and feelings. Alongside their instincts, they cannot help but follow.

People have the ability to know the difference between what's right and what's wrong. Dog's don't. Your dog will always choose to do the things they have been genetically programmed to do. Stuff that comes naturally to them.

You know what I mean right. Chasing off after next doors cat. Stealing the roast dinner joint off the kitchen worktop. Sniffing another dogs poop, barking when they're scared. You get the picture.

I bet you perform actions you've never given much thought to either.

Brushing your teeth. Combing your hair. Sticking the kettle on. Getting dressed. Always putting your shoes on before your coat. Collecting up the mail from the floor. Yeah? These are known as habits. These are things we can change whenever we want too.

How about sticking your hand out to break the impact of a fall? Yawning when you're tired. Sneezing when there's a tickle up your nozza. Being shocked and jumping at a loud noise or bang. Breathing.

These are known as instincts. These are things you and I both do without even thinking about them. Impulses and urges which are genetically programmed into us. Guess what, dogs have these too.

An all-time favourite quote of mine comes from Jean Donaldson:

'If you think about it, it's kind of a dirty trick to take a species that naturally chases moving objects, eats whatever it comes across, bites to argue (etc) and then announce all these as behaviour problems'

When human and canine behaviour collide, the collision can soon spiral out of control, and before you know it, you've got a ten-car pile-up on the motorway.

Once you accept your dog for what they are. Getting what you want from them isn't difficult at all.

"Because dogs live in the present. Because dogs don't hold grudges. Because dogs let go of all their anger daily, hourly, and never let it

fester. They absolve and forgive with each passing minute. Every turn of a corner is the opportunity for a clean slate. Every bounce of a ball brings joy and the promise of a fresh chase."

– Stephen Rowley

Chapter Two: Here's How To Create A Fearful Dog

There is no definitive answer as to why your dog became fearful. Not using a book anyway. However, there are a few factors I believe can increase the chances of them developing this type of bark. I have selected four things I consider to contribute towards this emotion presenting itself.

Barking is a natural thing for your dog to do. Other than on Lock Stock and two smoking barrels, I have never heard a dog quack. Nor have I heard them bah, moo or tweet twoo like an owl. A dog will bark.

Ain't no getting around it. How much they bark and with what intensity can quite quickly increase from a standard rate of barking communication, into an uncontrolled, deafening and confrontational mess though.

Let's look at the first one.

Draw Me, Like One Of Your French ...Bulldogs

Ever wondered why Golden Retrievers like to hold things in their mouth? Or why terriers love to sod off over the horizon in pursuit of a rabbit? Maybe you don't understand why your spaniel likes to dig up the garden and bury his toys?

The short and sweet of it is your dog was bred for a purpose. Yep, look down at your pooch now. What was the original job for them, way back when dogs were first created?

Genetics play a bigger part than you probably realise in your dog's behaviours. Here's a little origin story for you while they snore and fart at your feet.

Somewhere in Israel way back when. A 12,000-year-old skeleton of a man was found with its arms wrapped around the bony structure of a four to five-month-old dog pup. It's generally accepted these days; dogs have been domesticated for around 20,000-40,000 years.

Although we've been breeding dogs for many generations. Back then, breeds were more like types. Over the years, the domestication process has produced several physical changes. Including an array of breeds even I don't know the bloody names of.

I often have to ask myself these days with the puppies who enter my classroom what they are. Unless It's apparent of course. I do know my cockers from my collies and my westies from my huskies.

However, there is a much wider variety of dog breeds around these days. At one time, the categories and types were much smaller.

House or guardian dogs
Shepherd dogs
Sporting dogs
War dogs
Scent hounds.
Sighthounds.

With these 'types' they had specific roles to perform. Now naturally, I'm not going to go through each one. So, let's just concentrate on the guard dog. These are dogs who have been specifically bred to … guard. Who'd have thunked it!

How do you think a dog like this is going to effectively do their guarding role? Ten points toooooo GRIFINDORRR! Please tell me you've watched Harry Potter.

It's true! These dogs performed and were encourages to bark to fulfil the roles they were needed to. The best guard dogs were then bred again to produce even better, barking guard dogs and so on and so forth.

Skye and Hunter are German Shepherds and yeah, they alert bark when there is someone at the door. A natural thing for them to do. I doth laugh sometimes when I meet fellow guarding breed owners, and they say to me *'He's found his voice this week and started barking. What can I do about it?'*

Around 14-16 weeks of age, the dog do what the dog was bred to do. They hit their 'growing up stage,' and this is where instincts start to blossom. Dancing like thunder, singing in the rain and blooming like a flower. This can be a bit of a shock to some people.

Sure, barking is not classed as a desirable behaviour, but you know, dogs have been bred too and will bark. If you don't want them to bark then I'm in no way saying you can't teach them not too, but you must understand and accept it's ingrained in them. It's who they are.

Having the expectation, a dog should never bark will land you up shit's creek. It's like saying you don't want the cow to moo!

It's all about how we teach them to do something else instead of the barking which is gonna make a big difference here.

Even Bob The Builder Can't Fix This One

There are two points in the genetics aspect of the barking dog I'm going to share. Bad breeding is ever increasing, and it's unquestionably different today than it was ten to twenty years ago. There are still some exceptional breeders out there. Ones who work stupidly hard to ensure everything is right with the pregnancy and the pups have the ulti-mutt upbringing. See what I did there.

These breeders tend to have long waiting lists. Sometimes years in advance. They really do, do things properly.

Though today's society is, unfortunately, an on-demand one and people just don't have any god damn patience to wait anymore.

Want a pizza? Click a few buttons, await delivery. Like a song on the radio but don't know who sings it? You can find out and download it just by asking your phone. All before the songs finished playing on the radio. Want a new puppy? Just go online and order one.

'Wait, what??'

Yep, you can now order a puppy online. Fucking crazy if you ask me but on demand puppies buying services are out there. It's ridiculous.

Puppy farms are a real thing, and unfortunately, these puppies don't have a fraction of the care and health support the good breeders provide. You'll find them locked in small pen's; bitches unable to turn around. Fed once a day if they're lucky. Have no sunlight. They can't exercise and are highly stressed. The puppies are also subjected to this trauma. Never seeing the light of day until they are sold.

Although these conditions are disgraceful. Poorly bred puppies are also in ordinary people's homes. Doing so because they think their bitch needs to have puppies or they just wanted a bit of extra cash in their back pocket.

These puppies are already at a disadvantage. Don't even think about taking your puppy back to these kinds of breeders. They generally don't want to know.

I can often tell a poorly bred puppy or one who's socialisation stage hasn't been great when I see one. Those first few weeks of life and upbringing are the most important. If they don't get what they need, it can severely impact their behaviour.

I remember a puppy entering my classroom, ooh what maybe three to four years ago now. I always expect a level of nervousness in the first class from them all. It's a new environment, there other puppies around, it smells different, and it can be noisy if the lads are kicking the footballs around downstairs. My classroom can sometimes be the first experience a puppy has of being outside.

It doesn't take them long under my teaching to be comfortable and having fun, though. This is something I work hard at to achieve. The last thing I want is a stressed out and anxious puppy in training.

Unfortunately, sometimes puppies enter who are not doing well at all and I have to remove them from the hall. This particular one was too scared to move or come out for anything. Even with space away from the others, this puppy was not improving, and I sent her on to a behaviourist.

Before I did this, I asked a few questions and found out a little more about the puppies' upbringing. It wasn't good at all. Poor genetics means a puppy will already be wired up, so to speak, to be scared, anxious, fearful, and unable to cope. Generally leading on to barking. Some things you simply cannot fix, only ever manage.

Digger is one of those dogs. His socialisation stage was terrible. He was kept locked in a stable up until 16 weeks of age, before coming to us. I still have to manage and will continue to, until his dying day. Though you can always make improvements mind, it's not like you're doomed forever. It only goes back to having the consideration of where and what time you walk, so it's enjoyable for you and your dog. I do this with Digger all the time.

Next up! Fur Missiles!

'Stress is a precursor to fear, which basically means that if your dog's parents suffered stress through the pregnancy, then the puppies are much more vulnerable to having a fearful response. This also means that the puppies will not only have a lack of confidence, but they will also struggle to cope in a lot of situations'

Warning! Fur Missile Incoming!

The look of horror on my face when I hear these words must be quite apparent. *'I should probably socialise them more. They need to get used to it'*

'Nooooo. Stop! Right Now... thank you very much' Name that tune?

Socialisation is a massively misunderstood concept. When dogs bark through fear, they are automatically rewarded, and if you expose them to an environment where they will bark. It's going to increase your dogs barking.

Let's stick with your dog's perspective. The thing they are most scared of appears, they bark and then it goes away, doesn't it? Therefore, the barking, in your dog's head, has worked.

The postman delivering the mail. Other dogs enjoying their walk. Children heading to school. Traffic driving on the road. Get the picture?

Remembering me telling you how I made so many mistakes with Titon when he started barking? Well, this is one of the things I did, which I thought would improve his barking. I set off into the town with my boy in the back, heading straight for the populated dog areas of Buxton. Pavilion Gardens it's called.

'The Pavilion Gardens is a beautiful historic venue dating back to 1871 which superbly shows off the Victorian splendour of Buxton. Set within 23-acres of magnificent landscaped gardens and play areas the venue provides the perfect setting for fun and relaxing family days

out, with great food and drink, shopping and over 100 events and festivals throughout the year.'

It is quite a sight to see. I used to work in England oldest hotel. The Old Hall Hotel, which has included some notable guests or the years including Mary Queen of Scots herself. The hotel not only stands as one of the town's most popular places to stay and it's situated directly opposite the Pavilion Gardens and the famous Buxton Opera House. I'd like to say I met Mary Queen of Scots, but obviously, I didn't. I'm only 31.

Anyway, my experience of 'socialising' my fearful barking dog didn't go to plan at all.

Dogs have something called a fight or flight survival mode. When you put a fearful dog into a situation to try and get them used to something. One of two things can happen.

With Titon, I got out of the van and hooked him up on the lead. As we were heading towards the gardens, I could see people and dogs dotted everywhere, the birds relaxing on the water's edge and the sound of the children screaming and laughing in the play area. Naturally, I went the other way to the children. They scare me, and I shut down in their presence. Which I'll come on to shortly.

Off we went and Titon seemingly okay. We made our way towards the water to go and sit on one of the benches so he could see what was going on and 'get used to it' No sooner had I set foot on the track, I was met with pulling. Bloody hell, *'Cchhh pack it in lad.'* To no avail. Then came

67

the lunging at the birds, the barking, and the advances towards approaching dogs.

I didn't stay long. But I had one hell of a task turning him around and heading back to where I was parked. It was a nightmare! Remember me telling you about my ordeal with the big black spider and the panic-stricken dance moves I made? This is how the erm, walk went with Titon. He totally freaked out and all he really learned from this day was his barking kept working.

The birds flew off into the water. The children, well we weren't close enough to them but the dogs and people he barked at went on their way, and out of his. Great, back to the drawing board then.

There is another approach a fearful barking dog can take, and it's something I saw a lot of at a dog show I recently went too. I want you to take your biggest fear. No guesses needed on what I'm going to use. Right, have you got it?

This time, instead of there only being one of these things, there are hundreds. You are put on a lead and forced to enter the shit-scary realms of your fears. Trapped with no viable way of getting out. These things are within striking distance, should you choose to lash out, but because there are so many of them, the survival response your fear responses tell you to use is to completely freeze.

You are unable to move a muscle and are now in an extreme state of fear. Your body has quite literally shut down or is shutting out the threats. If you run or scream out, it might get you. It might even touch you. *'Eurgh!'*

You're flooded and have no idea what to do.

The socialisation concept is dangerous when done wrong. Be it with a puppy or a recovering barking dog. Forcing your dog to do things they are not comfortable with is called Flooding. Which is like the Ronseal adverts slogan. It does exactly what it says on the tin.

Your dog is drowning in a sea of fear, unable to escape. Completely overwhelmed and genuinely petrified. When dogs shut down, to the untrained human eye, it can appear the 'training' is working, and they are getting used to it. Though the next time, they encounter the scary thing in less overwhelming environments. The barking will be worse.

Exactly what happened with Titon. The next time we were out walking and back on the quieter beaten tracks, the distractions we encountered a distraction. It left me once again hanging on to the lead, giving it everything I'd got strength wise in me to prevent him from getting hold of the other dog and person.

The moral of the story. Don't flood your dog. It doesn't work.

Correct socialisation is described as follows:

'Socialisation is where puppies and dogs are exposed to different environments, and social situations in a positive way, and they view that as a good thing. This is crucial in promoting confidence and reducing the risk of behavioural issues, later in life'

It's unfair and unethical to presume your dog will just be okay. Always think like your dog and from their perspective. Take the preventative steps and increase your distance away, like I took with Titon. Avoid what they fear, until we get to the section of this book where I will show you a better way of successfully helping your dog to overcome them.

Life Is A Fight, But Not Everyone Is A Fighter

Being bullied can make you feel miserable and powerless. Bullying affects each person in different ways. Common feelings include ashamed, hopeless and stuck, like it's your fault, alone with no one to help you. Depressed and rejected. Unsafe and afraid. Confused and stressed out.

Basically, being bullied sucks!

It's hurtful, scary, and confusing. When bullying is aggressive and physical, it can be dangerous. When it's emotional, like name-calling, or cyberbullying, it's easy to feel alone.

Fortunately, I was never bullied as a youngster. I was one of those kids who was quiet but confident. I can recall another student coming over to me one day and asking whether they thought I was cool because I was smoking.

Before this, I had voiced my strong opinions to another student thinking it was funny to put her hamster in the microwave where its feet turned black. I think I called her a fucking idiot and that she should be ashamed of herself and to never cross paths with me again.

And with this, came the backlash of standing up for yourself and what you believe in. Oh yeah, this kid got right up in my face at the back of the French buildings where I was smoking. So close I could see the blackheads on her nose and felt the spatter of her spit hitting my face as she yelled at me.

'It's cooler than animal abuse,' I replied. Dead calm and collected like.

I wasn't afraid of many things. So much so, I wouldn't even hesitate in scrapping. Which is what was coming. I watched as she took a step back, huffing and laughing to her peers behind. Me ever intently watching and waiting for the swing.

And it came. She turned further away from me, and I saw her right elbow crease and swing behind her. Then came the step forward toward me, which is where I shifted my position to the left side, grabbed her arm and using her own body weigh against her. Then I drop kicked her to the floor and looked down.

I'm not a violent person promise, but I will defend myself.

As puppies, a lot of people can opt for showing their new family member everything over what it really a short space of time. We are encouraged to 'socialise' our dogs to anything we want them to be okay with as an adult.

Being okay with other dogs is a big one here. Following on from the last section, it is automatically presumed a dog needs to have other dog friends to be friendly and socialised. Willingly allowing dogs to play with each other off the lead and regularly is the first port of call.

'No! No! Nooooo! Lord Jesus if you really exist up there, then please send immediate help!'

Okay, here's the deal. Allowing free play between your dogs and others can cause way more problems than it ever does good and it's worth.

Your dog can either become bullied. Or be the bully.

For the purpose of this book, I'm only going to tell you about the dogs who get bullied. The bullies' part will go into another book I will write.

Now then, here's where it gets a little tricky. If you have two healthy, confident, and outgoing dogs, who can play nicely together. Taking the play in turns like. Not bounding around with each other like an out of control young driver tear-arsing around in the supermarket car parks after hours, in their supped-up Golfs. I love nothing more than seeing proper play between dogs.

Though this is similar to seeing an Albini Alligator waltzing through the high-street doing it's shopping these days. With approximately a dozen left in the world, finding two evenly matched dogs playing fairly is just as rare.

Here's what tends to happen.

You get one dog who is head over heels in love with playing, and with this, they get mega rough with the other. Then we have the other dog who is hating every single minute of it and trying to get away. Which gets missed. Who enjoys being used as a living breathing bouncy castle?

Hunter had a fantastic socialisation stage. I run puppy classes and I'm a fully qualified dog training instructor, so I knew what I needed to do. Plus, I had the resources available to me to get this phase right. Positively showing him the world and always taking things at his pace.

I used to use Hunter as my puppy demo dog in the classes, which was great for me. I could show what I was teaching and teach my puppy at the same time. Result!

Though even with all of this at my fingertips, things still went wrong for us. He had a minor incident in the classroom after the class. I always crated him while the others were leaving, and then rereleased him as I was packing down. This was mainly to save me sweeping, and he thoroughly enjoyed cleaning up the left-over treats and crumbs on the floor.

As I was putting away the chairs and was in the store cupboard, I heard the classroom door bang. I came out and looked over to see a client coming back in with her puppy. Hunter already on his way over to greet them.

Before I knew it, this dog was jumping and play fighting all over my puppy. I panicked a little because this was not a behaviour, I wanted Hunter to learn. He was going to be a big dog and A: I didn't want him free playing plus, B: I didn't want any learned uncertainties should he get hurt or dislike the engagement.

I instantly took a handful of treats to Hunter's nose and attempted to lure him away. The other puppy began to try harder to keep playing as Hunter was following me. I took to picking this puppy up because Hunters face was screaming '*Okay, fuck off now, I am not enjoying this anymore*'

This wasn't the main incident in Hunter becoming a fearful barking dog, but it's an example of how easy it can be and only take one incident to ruin your dog's outlook on things.

Dogs don't need other dog friends.

If your dog has suffered and become a bully through free play, they could well have already learned, *this* is something to be cautious of. Be it another dog, a child, an adult rough handling them. Whatever. But other dogs are the topic of this chapter.

It isn't written in the Canine Bible of Friendliness your dog has to get on with everything they encounter. I quite like my own space with my select group of friends. Often opting for quiet rural pub locations with a roaring fire and an ability to catch up and chat together.

For me, a meal and a few drinks I would be happy with. Though some people prefer busier places with loud music and people throwing up in the nearest back alley. We all have opinions and preferences in what we do and don't enjoy. Your dog is the same.

Prevention is key.

'He is your friend, your partner, your defender, your dog. You are his life, his love, his leader. He will be yours faithful and true to the last beat of his heart. You owe it to him to be worthy of such devotion' - Anonymous

Chapter Three: Why Being Wrong, Is Right

It's okay to be wrong. We learn from making mistakes. Most people have a misunderstanding as to why their dog is barking. You are here to read and learn where you may have gone wrong. This is a smart mindset to be in.

Taking steps to fix a problem you are having, shows courage, intellect, and open-mindedness to trying new things. In seeking a solution to improve your dog ownership life, it shows responsibility, and with this an ability to amend and make things so much better.

It's okay if you've tried and failed. These mistakes are the learning blocks you can carry forward with you to now getting things back on track. Perhaps you've worked with a dog trainer before, but it didn't solve your problem? Maybe you didn't give the training the time and everything it needed to work effectively?

Giving up is a natural feeling to have, especially when dealing with these kinds of dogs. All of the things you have tried and potentially failed with is a considerable step to now moving in a direction and into a world which will help you should you follow and practice it correctly.

When you can take steps to admit you have been wrong, only then can we start to re-build things.

As I've already said, I fucked up with Titon majorly. It would have been easy for me to give up and hide him away on the open fields and out of sight of everyone forever.

But how far would this have got me when the time came for me to move. To a village, with people and stuff in it.

I'll tell you now, it would have been a complete nightmare. Don't become rooted in self-righteousness, though. These are people I just cannot help.

Arrogance is a funny thing. Arrogant people think they are always right. This type of temperament is only going to set these types up to fail. Whereas we want success. If I had a quid for every time, I saw people sharing their opinions on fixing a barking dog on social media, the advice is wrong. I'd be a multi-millionaire by now.

Recommending all sorts of punishment-based equipment and techniques to 'fix' the problem. Sorry to say, there is never a quick fix in proper dog training. Keep in mind we are looking at the emotional side of things, not just the not barking. Bad emotion = lousy behaviour. Good, happy feeling = better responses.

What's even more comical with these 'types' is the tone of morality; they dish back replies when you share your opinion on what the person should really be doing. I.e., Getting professional help and suggesting to them these previous things are wrong and potentially dangerous to do.

They don't like it.

They begin to get defensive and then get personal towards you. A clear indicator of them being wrong. Defensive people have difficulty taking responsibility for their actions and often feel uncomfortable being 'wrong.' It's because accepting responsibility would make them feel as if they have failed.

Defensive behaviour might stem from a tough childhood or traumatic past, which can make a person more likely to "react through a negative lens," Then it becomes a bad habit as an adult.

They effectively bully you into believing them. Displaying emotions of shock, you would even think about questioning what they were saying. You know the type.

- Reward-based training is ineffective, it's making dogs worse.
- I've been training this way for years, and it's always worked

- I'm 65 and have had dogs all my life

'Big. Fat. Lol'

What a load of shite. I've been female all my life, this doesn't mean I can proclaim to be any sort of gynaecologist.

It really is wrong, to always think you are right. And there is no point in trying to talk to them. You can lead a horse to water and all that...

Moving on. When you accept and take on board, it's okay to be wrong, something magical begins to happen. As the unethical and pretentious door closes, a new one activates and opens. Entering a world, you have never experienced before.

Anything and everything you wanted to achieve starts to become possible. It's now within easy reach, and you can conquer your goals.

'If you do what you've always done, you'll get what you've always gotten.'

This can sometimes be an overwhelming world to enter at first. There is so much information to take in and re-learn. You have no way of knowing if it's really going to work, then you find it does for a bit. Then perhaps your dog reverts to barking again. But we put these steps in to place for valid reasons.

It's always going to take longer and more work to fix something that's already been working for your dog. It's merely a habit you need to un-do.

If you listen, learn, and give this everything you've got, you will have a much higher chance of things being amazing. The success you seek can transform into a reality.

Dare I say much quicker than if you think you are always right. Going back to things you have been previously doing and getting no-where with is simply an old habit you haven't yet mastered in ridding.

A fear lies within us all. Doing the unknown or stepping out of your comfort zone can be a worry. Bringing a heightened risk to your thought processes. But by going against the grain and doing things differently. Putting in the work required and sticking with the program. You will have much more success further down the line.

You won't have to continually tell your dog to shut up. Nor will you have to torture yourself before going out the front door with them. And you can forget about being dragged from pillar to post. Wouldn't this be nice?

There are unfamiliar ideas in this book. At least two main points you may think are ridiculous. Perhaps you believe there is more. It isn't something to be judged by you yet, though. If you haven't trialled or practiced them yet, how can you?

The first thing to put those unsure crinkles on your forehead is in how I work with a dog. I genuinely believe handlers are causing more problems than they should be. You need to chill out and quit telling your dog off for things. You're wasting your time.

The second. If you ever get the opportunity to see me working with a dog in person, or in my online courses, you will rarely hear me talking to them. Heck no, it just ruins the training. Much better to put up and shut up, instead of talking to your dog like they understand what you are saying to them.

Here's something for you to think about. How many times do you have to ask your dog to sit? To lie down. To wait for their dinner. To stop pulling. To quit barking.

If it's any more than once, then somethings going wrong. If you don't have to ask them at all and they just do it, then bravo my friend.

The sprinkling of pixie dust on better managing your barking dog is not to engage or express too many words with them. This brings the best results. Instead, you can work in silence. Using only your body movements to get precisely what you want from your dog.

How can you change your own behaviour, to help transform your dogs?

If you aren't prepared to make an effort and improve yourself, then the solutions you are seeking simply don't exist. If you can't remain quiet and calm yourself, how can you expect your dog to?

"You will never reach your destination, if you stop and throw stones at every dog that barks" -Winston Churchill

The Role Of The Teacher

I remember when I was learning about dog training. One of the tasks we were given involved being put into pairs, with four or five small handheld objects between us. The point of this game was for one person to arrange a sequence of the items, on how we would like for them to be moved. No verbal instructions were given to the other person.

I had sorted out in my head how I wanted my training partner to pick them up and in what order. She struggled and stared intently at me to see if I was giving away any facial clues via eyesight towards the intended item or not. When it was my go, I can't describe to you how frustrating it was. A complete head fuck.

With no guidance, support, or instructions, a task as simple as this one was the ruination of my patience. This relates well to how we teach our dogs, or should I say, how we test them. When we begin training them, if we aren't providing clear instructions to follow, it can soon become horrendously tricky for your dog to interpret what it is you want them to do. And almost impossible for them to succeed.

The task demonstrated how confusing and easy it is for your dog to get. We expect too much from them, far too soon. We test when we should be teaching. In the activity, when I got selected the incorrect item, I felt defeated. Frustrated, and for some reason, I looked around the room for other support and guidance.

When you ask your dog to sit, does he fully understand it? Can he perform it anywhere you go? Or do you have to ask him several times?

A sit is a simple behaviour, one of the first things a dog learns to do. But when you look at the simple actions, and your dog cannot adequately perform them the first time, when asked. How can we expect them to master the harder and more emotionally based behaviours such as staying quiet or coping around things they find scary? Answer: We can't.

How do you complete a marathon without training and preparation? Again, you can't. Therefore, you should not expect your dog to be able to control their emotions if you haven't put any time into teaching them, it's okay, and they've nothing to worry about.

The dogs in my experience are easy to teach. I find it's the humans who take a little longer.

The more I think about it, I'm not a dog trainer at all. I'm Mrs. Do-Little... okay just playing. I'm a people trainer. This soon gets recognised when I'm teaching. My work has been viewed as magic. Similar to an illusion, people struggle to comprehend. Those problems and challenges people have been facing with their dog, disappear super quickly when I take hold of the lead and show them. Why is this?

I went to Ireland earlier this year for a wedding. We arrived on a Friday, and I totally bailed out early as I was exhausted from the weeks work, plus getting everything ready with the dogs on going away. I never fully appreciate how much I do until I have to hand over to someone else.

On the Saturday, we arrived at the church sat through the ceremony before getting on a coach and being taken to Falcon Manor. This place was grand, just like something out of Game of Thrones. Ancient with a massive entrance hall, grounds filled with acres of trees, land, and views to die for. It was a pretty picture.

As we entered, there were drinks on arrival and a gathering of guests congregating in the reception. I heard what I thought was an owl. Surely not. My thoughts turned out to be correct, and through the crowds of people, I saw a man with a glove on, and this mahoosive creature sat on his arm, throwing out consistent and repetitive squarks.

After photos in the reception and me posing with a glass of prosecco. I didn't drink it, I'd have been on the floor quicker than a shoot-off between two cowboys. We arrive at the bar area. Shocker, I know.

It quickly filled with guests and got really hot in there, so I decided to head back out to the entrance hall to cool off and rest my feet. Those shoes I was made to wear were a killer. If I'd have had my way, I'd have been more than happy in my dog trainer boots.

As I sat on the grand reception chair, I watched on to find two more handlers and their birds, wink wink, hanging around talking to guests about the species on their arm. The man with the falcon was now only a few feet away from me, and we caught each other's eye. I could drift off into love at first sight story there, but I wouldn't be talking about the chap.

I hesitantly got up, feeling the pain return into my feet to chat with him about the falcon, he went on to tell me all sorts of facts. So much so, I couldn't tell you half of them there were so many. Though I do remember him explaining the hunting process and how the bird could reach speeds up to 200mph on a downward spiral. Imagine that!

The falcon had what I can only describe as a head helmet on, let's call it his invisibility cloak. This was to settle the bird in the busy environment, preventing any stress to the animal but also to prevent it from flapping and trying to getaway.

After a few minutes, I asked if I could hold the bird. By this time, my sister had joined us, and I gave her my phone for an obligatory falcon selfie. As he positioned the bird on my arm, he continued telling us facts and stories about this magnificent predator.

I was flicking my head between the falcon and this chap, and as I was listening to him, I noticed him do a double-take at my hand. Being an intuitive being, I instantly noticed his facial reactions and thought, *'Oh shit, what's the matter.'*

Had the bird shit on my arm? Did I do something wrong? As I turned my head down to look, I saw the bird has tucked his right leg up into his feathers and was resting on one leg. A little like how a horse takes the weight off their legs while they're sleeping. Which I didn't think a great deal too, to be honest. I expected the worst or maybe to find it hanging upside down like a bat. I dunno.

'This is really interesting' he said. *'I've only ever seen this once before, and it was about 4 years ago.'*

Okay... what does this mean? Pondering and zoning in on his words over the hustle and bustle of the busy crowds, I listened properly. He went on to say how this behaviour meant the bird was 110% relaxed, effectively falling asleep. Which was rare, especially in a busy and somewhat stressful environment for the animal.

It was something about the person the bird picked up on. Something relaxing and being at ease with them. A falcon quite literally fell asleep on my hand. Maybe my Mrs. Do-Little joke earlier is correct. Hmm...

After departure and back on English soil, I reflected on this more, and I realised a lot of what I do comes naturally and is automated within my day to day routine and temperament. I'm cool, calm, and collected by nature, and this is something I can often struggle to teach to others.

It isn't impossible to teach, but it's more a state of mind than it is a physical training technique. The main things I reflected on and believed contributed to the snoring falcon were this.

I didn't bother the bird; I wasn't ruffling up his feathers or prodding and poking around. I opted for listening and leaving him alone. Sure, I touched his feathers when prompted to do so by the chap, but other than this. No contact at all.

I also remained incredibly calm, even after it fluttered randomly at me in the beginning and put extra frizz into my hair after spending an age straightening in. Big sigh. But yeah, my emotional state of calm clearly transferred. The handler suggested I go back to the UK and go for handling training. He effectively told me to go and get a job with them. He was so amazed.

Being able to stay calm in the presence of a strong, noisy, lunging, barking dog is up there as a hard thing to do. But like anything in life, it's a skill. One which needs practicing. Take note of when your dog is completely relaxed. I'm talking on their back, legs in the air kind of relaxed. For some, it may be when they're inside and cuddled up to you, for others it may be when you leave them alone. Take note of this.

Going back to dogs, when I work with them owner's jaws have opened and dropped to the floor quicker than the excited 'Wolf Howl' scene from the film 'The Mask'

'Can you come and live with us for a few months?'
'Are you a dog whisperer?'
'What is this wizardry?!'

Are all statements I hear regularly. I don't have any magical Harry Potter, Bertie Botts treats on offer. I don't cast an 'Expecto Patronum' spell over the dog. I do something much easier than this.

I speak to the dog in a language they understand.

Most people forget this is a partnership and should always be a team effort at any given time of day. Training isn't just a hat you put on and wear when somethings going wrong. This is a lifestyle.

Once you embrace it and begin to see the benefits of working in a calm, kind, consistent, and patient manner. You can change things and all for the better.

Have You Got Your Head In The Clouds?

It's easy to see your dog as an annoying and sometimes irritating little creature. Even though they do have some frustrating habits, some sending my face into a rage and cringing overdrive. I always let out a little chuckle afterward to remind myself, my human-ness has briefly overtaken my understanding of the dog.

Here's a quick task for you. I want you to take a pen and paper and simply watch your dog for three, 5-minute intervals. Sit down with a brew and make a note of what your dog does during this time. Obviously, if you choose a time when they're sleeping and do all three of these viewings inside the house, it's going to be a pretty dull activity.

Unless you go super dog, owner style and count the number of times their paw twitches while they were catching imaginary rabbits. Or how many times their eyes blinked when you looked at them.

Do this activity when there is nothing too distracting for them, and it's pretty clear, but I must state it. Don't do this when they're barking. Trying to take notes and hang onto them is almost impossible.

Where do they look? How were their ears positioned? What mischief did they get up to? When did they choose to settle? How many times did they look directly at you?

Don't speak to or look directly at them while doing this. You're going to need to look at them for sure, but if they look at you, simply drop your head to your piece of paper and wait until they go off and do their own things again. No staring contests here, please!

In doing this activity and really watching your dog's behaviour, perhaps won't mean a great deal to you right now, but as we go through the book. Understanding your dog's body language is going to be a crucial element in understanding what they are really saying. Not how you perceive it to be. I'm talking about dog language.

I'm always looking down at the dog I have, rarely looking out at what's around me. This may seem like a strange concept to you, but I can get everything I need in my training sessions by watching how the dog is feeling.

Sure, I have to watch where I'm walking or what I'm about to walk into. I've been known to walk into signposts and dustbins sticking out before mind. But when I do this, I find my anxiety and worries dramatically decrease.

You have to be on some sort of watch mode while you're out, I get that. Though when you do it too often, it can affect your emotional mindset. By always watching out for what's coming, you're thinking about what can go wrong. But in watching and engaging with your dog more, it can release those worries and uncertainties because you haven't got your head in the clouds.

This is something I do most days now, with my own or with client's dogs. I first properly started restricting my anxious mindset when I had Hunter, though. I found I shouldn't watch him too much in case I increased his anxiety, but I could glance down and watch him without causing too much of an intrusion but also so I could see how he was feeling.

Was he sniffing to take in scent, or was it because he was unsure? Did he stop and freeze because there was a dog ahead or was it more of a curiosity or *'Who's there'* movement? German Shepherds are aloof and alert by nature, but with Hunter, it could also mean *'OMFG I'm going to die'*

I found by watching my dog, he would tell me much more about what was going on around me. They're incredibly in tune with their environment, you know.

The posture of your dog can change, and when you take note and really look at what body language they are displaying, it's a game-changer.

I've put together a relaxed and fearful body language diagram for you on my website. I'll be going more into fearful body language, in the Fear Barkers Body Guide, but to compare and visually, simply head to www.3sts.co.uk

He's Not Protecting You!

He's protecting me. A statement I hear a lot, but sorry to be the bearer of bad news, dogs are selfish. Fearful barkers don't bark to protect you, they do it to protect themselves.

Think about it for a second. Something they're shit scared of is in close quarters, they're on the lead with no way of escaping and heading back to the two different kinds of fear responses a dog can use, is either fear submission or... you got it! Fear defensive.

A.K.A *This is scary, back off now or I will protect myself!*

Dogs don't bark to be a pain in your ass. It's more a case of them being put into a situation they just don't like. Then when they begin to express their emotions, it can become similar to Chinese whispers.

They are saying one thing; you interpret it as another. It gets passed down the line to family members, and before you know it, your dog's original emotional intentions are nothing more than the embers phasing out in the fire.

Alongside mindset, this is another thing I find hard to get across to people. My views and opinions aren't always met with agreement, and the human brain is designed to believe only what you want it to believe. This is because people spend so long thinking this is why it's hard to override the original thoughts and replace them with the new ones.

To get a more accurate representation of what your dog is really saying to. Not only do you have the pen and paper exercise to do, plus the visual body language diagrams of relaxed and fearful body language, but now we are going to currently identify what YOUR dog is saying.

I am a huge fan of recording my training sessions. Not just to pass onto clients, but so I can look back on them and double-check everything was as it should have been. It's insanely difficult and almost impossible to record your dog while they're barking, on your own. So, you're gonna need to go I wanna be a millionaire style here and phone a friend, acquiring an extra pair of hands for this next task.

- Set up a situation where you know your dog is likely to bark. Be this with the help of another dog owner or someone interpreting the arrival of a delivery driver. Whatever it is.
- Don't intentionally scare your dog but be ready to record them via a video camera when they start barking. Most smartphones have decent video recorders on them.
- I'm talking no more than a minute here, which will feel like a long time, but once the recording has stopped, get your dog out of the situation, so they stop barking
- Then offer support until they are calm again. Not while they are barking. Only when they are more

relaxed and listening to you. I don't want you getting any snaps or redirections, okay.

Once you've got your recording and settled down your dog. I want you to play it back and watch it several times over. Watch their body language and write down what you see. There are also plenty of slow-motion editors and programs out there too if you struggle to see what's happening in fast mode.

I want you to tally up your own dog's behaviour against the 'Fear Barkers Body Guide' below.

This has an importance rating of 100!! You have to identify why your dog is barking.

The Fear Barkers Body Guide

- Ears flat back
- Hackles raised (this is the fur on the back of the neck and hips)
- Low body posture
- Lips curled
- Pupils dilated
- Tail tucked with little or no movement (the tail is not always tucked right under)
- Corner of the mouth pulled back
- Nose wrinkled
- High Pitched bark
- Long series of barking, sometimes ending in a howl
- Restless, running back and forth.

This bark is all about making something go away.

After looking at this list, I can already see you thinking to yourself, how the feck am I supposed to see dilated pupils or the wrinkled nose. Don't panic, I'm not expecting you too. Let's be realistic. Even through the use of a recording, you may well struggle to see these things. This is why professionals should be bought into A: do a proper assessment and history of the dog and B: provide you with a detailed and personalised training plan for your dog.

I haven't dragged you all this way to not give you something to look for though, and I'm aware not everybody can afford the costs of a professional trainer and behaviourist.

Instead, what I would like you to focus on are just a few of those body language signs by following my HELPS formula.

HELPS:

- Hackles Raised
- Ears flat back
- Low tail
- Posture
- Sound of the bark

There are varying degrees of fearful responses, some ranging from slightly worried. Others escalating to full-on panic. You can clearly hear the panic and fear in your dog from the high-pitched sound of the bark, but you need to look at the whole picture.

It is in these panicked times where your dog will not be able to think correctly. Think back to your fear and being surrounded and flooded so much by it, where you couldn't physically think straight. Too concerned with surviving and getting the fuck out of there alive. This is how to imagine your dog's state of mind.

If you keep an eye out on the HELPS formula and be aware of your dog's emotional state, things will start to become easier for you. Nobody in their right mind wants to think about or see their dog struggling and being so scared. So support them. Don't cover it up with excuses like they're protecting me, or they should know better by now.

When you start to see these signals and knowing what you know now, those feelings of anger and frustration you hold get blown away. Being replaced with concern and additional support in helping your dog through the trauma, they are experiencing.

Soon, you will be a fully-fledged kinder, patient, and supportive addition to your fearful dog's life. Something these dogs are in desperate need of.

Dogs can become afraid or nervous about things at any given time in their lives. Puppies tend to be more prone to developing fear-based behaviours, but it can and does happen in older dogs too. Either via medical problems, a learned response, or perhaps signs of dementia creeping in.

'If a dog will not come to you after having looked you in the face, you should go home and examine your conscience' -Woodrow Wilson

Don't You Wanna Grow Up To Be Just Like Me?!

'I get a clean shave, bathe, go to a rave, die from an overdose, and dig myself up out of my grave. My finger won't go down, how do I wave. And this is how I'm supposed to teach kids how to behave.'

These are the lyrics from Eminem's tune, Role Model. The dog trainers' job is lovely, seriously I love my job more than chocolate and cups of coffees, and when people hear what it is, I do for a living, I hear the same things.

'Oh, I bet that's lovely'
'I'd love to work outside all day with dogs'
'Aren't you lucky'

And yes, I am. But with this, I think sometimes people think my job is easy. Perhaps they believe I stand in a field all day just chucking a tennis ball around or letting the dogs pull me up the hills of which stand tall in the Peak District. I dunno, but this idyllic vision of working with dogs isn't always so pleasant.

I've had many people approach me for work or work experience in the past, some going as far as coming to one of my classes and then they go and do something ridiculous. Like not even silly, it's more dangerous than anything.

They wake up one morning, decide they hate the job they're in, set up a website, head out into the world, and tell people they are a dog trainer. Yikes!

As much as I love my job and a lot of the time, it doesn't feel like a job. It is hard work. To do what I do, and do it properly involves more than just sticking a lead on a dog and going to a field for an hour throwing tennis balls about. You would never find me doing this.

You also wouldn't find me messing about on my phone while I have a dog in my care. Nor would you see me with a group of dogs being dragged down the street and allowing them to meet and greet anything and anyone they came across. You certainly won't see me letting them off the lead and doing whatever the hell they wanted to be doing.

Why? Because I know this can quickly ruin a dog's temperament and training with one wrong move.

Some people, however, don't take into consideration their limitations. I know full well what I can and can't do with dogs. Anything too severe behaviourally for me gets passed onto someone who can help. I only work with dog's I know I can help.

The dog walking and training trade is super unregulated, and people see it as easy money. This is where more and more problems are arising for dogs and their owners.

I received a message one day asking about spaces in my training classes. I was happy to share further details of the course and allocate a space, but I had this niggling feeling. You know when you get a gut instinct and an intuition something isn't quite right?

Then came a second message a couple of weeks later asking about the behaviour of a dog and what I'd do about it. I didn't answer. Then, get this. I see a post on a dog walkers group page stating a serious injury had been obtained and this person warning others locally his dog was dangerous.

It turned out, after a little digging around, this dog was scared of men and was a Jack Russell Terrier. I know how feisty this breed can be. Anyway, as the plot thickens, this person had taken on the dog as a training job. A man. And for the dog to cause such severe wounds, though I don't know exactly what was done, it told me he didn't know what he was doing.

As a result, if the dog hadn't learned to bite before, they had now. Here are my congratulations to you. Naht! Creating more problems in the barking dog world is up there as a big, big problem.

So many people focus on the behaviour they want, as opposed to the emotion the dog has, that is preventing the desired response from occurring. If a dog fears man, what don't we do?

Correct, put them into a situation they are afraid of before they are ready to cope with it. Always think about how your dog is really feeling and avoid the dog bite assessment on whether your dog gets prosecuted for something they don't have to.

It's nice to think of the dog training job as a good job, and it is. Please remember we have read hundreds of articles, trained for hours on end, been given additional help and support from our mentors, attended seminar after seminar, completed assignment after assignment. To get to the reputable and trustworthy standard, we are at today.

'Dog's lives are too short. Their only fault, really' Agnes Turnbull

Chapter Four: The Criminal Chaos You Are Creating Right Now

We've all made mistakes in life. Me more than most. In this section, I wanted to bust a few myths and share more of the errors I have made, which set my training back further. Changing human behaviour is hard. If you think about a habit you have, come on spill the beans...

A bad habit I have is not eating correctly. When I was a chef, I was constantly nit-picking at foods in the kitchen, and rarely eating a proper meal. Some days, mostly when I'd worked around the clock day in day out surrounded by food. I would get so sick of seeing it, I wouldn't want to eat at all.

When I reduced my catering hours, and then eventually came out of it altogether, this habit I'd evolved into didn't pass. To this day, I am still a complete nightmare with food. At the start of this year, one of my personal goals was to sustain a better diet. I'm active enough in my work and my energy levels soon drain when I've been out training for a while.

Do you know how insanely difficult I've been finding this? I speak in the present because it's still something I'm trying to master. I've been with the group for almost 6months now, and I'm still struggling to successfully keep on track with what I have to do numbers-wise and add into the diet week by week.

Something so simple as eating the way the program has been designed, and here's me having to try really hard to even remember doing it!

Old habits can be challenging to break, and healthy habits are often harder to develop than we would like. Ever heard the phrase 'nothing in life worth having, is ever easy?' It's harder because the behavioural patterns you and I repeat most often, are those that are etched into our brains.

How many times did your dog bark this week? How many times have they performed and repeated the behaviour? How long has this been a habit for them?

Here's some good news for you though, because just as we can develop and maintain new habits, so can your dog. Even long-term habits such as my terrible eating patterns, ones that are quite detrimental to a person's health and well-being can be shaken with enough determination and following a smart approach.

Even though I haven't cracked the plate building habits, I'm being taught. I've definitely improved. I eat breakfast most mornings, I have a new pattern of making sure I go to the village shop when I finish working, to pick up something to eat. It may not be in line with the healthy options and as nutrias as the group recommends just yet, but I'm eating. And it's a step in the right direction.

When you begin to teach your dog the new habits you'd like to see more of, sure it ain't gonna happen overnight, but there is no reason or excuse as to why you can't see some progress. You won't know until you try and to try let's look at changing your habits first.

Forgive Me, Father, For I Have Sinned

Picture the scene.

You are out with your friends and aren't too keen on large crowds of people. On holiday once, you got your stuff knicked from your handbag and lost some valuable possessions. Naturally, you are anxious and aware of it happening again. Large crowds heighten this fear.

Your friends are desperate to see a band playing tonight, and they're only playing a few miles away from you. You aren't overjoyed with the news, but nod and smile politely agreeing to go along.

When the time comes for the concert, you enter and keep a good firm grip of your bag. Double-checking it's still closed and safe. The crowds begin to increase, and you soon find yourself trapped between several men on a stag due. To the left, you see a group of youngsters with hoods and tracksuit bottoms hanging under their arse cheeks.

Your apprehension and anxiety rise and starts to become out of control. The fear of what could happen is taking over you.

Somebody pushed you! Is this a decoy in getting hold of your belongings? Instinctively you spin around, give them a powerful and angry look. Then feel your bag being tugged away in another direction and you flip out. Shouting and panicking.

Confused and shocked, the other party gets defensive. Shouting back at you at how you could think such a thing. You get so angry you begin pushing and shoving each other, roaring in each other's faces.

A temper tantrum. But what did it solve? You allowed your emotions to get the better of you before actually finding out what was going on. They weren't trying to steal your handbag, it just caught in their clothing and got stuck.

Your logical, thinking brain has gone. Your emotional mind in play, instead.

Past experiences can do this to us. We know of the risks and threats around because it's embedded in our brains, and fear takes over us to keep us safe. Survival mode.

Canine behaviour is closely linked to and influenced by emotions; just as human behaviour is. If you lash out and shout at your dog for the unwanted responses, it's only gonna make things worse.

How easy is it to tell off your dog, though? Fucking hell, easier than spreading butter onto bread sometimes. Guess who's been guilty of this. Yessums. Moi.

I've told you about doing things wrong with Titon, and shouting at him was one of them. But do you know what, fast forward a good few years. I've still been guilty of this with another dog. One in-particular.

Digger.

This lad came into my life, and I'll be honest when I say this, unnecessarily. My partner at the time had always wanted a border terrier. Who was silly enough to go out and get one for him? I had always been the keeper of German Shepherds. Dogs who want to be with you, are one owner dogs, listen, are easy enough to train.

Don't fuck off and ignore you at the sight of something furry running across the horizon. Don't catch said furry thing and then start to kill it. German Shepherds, or at least the ones I've had, don't shred and eat your flooring and wallpaper into tiny particles, bathing in it when you arrive home. Like a multi-millionaire taking a bath in all his cash.

Oh yeah, that's what I came back to one day. At the time, I had three jobs. I was a Monday to Friday dog walker, a chef by night and a kennel assistant Saturday and Sunday daytime. I was fortunate enough to be able to take my dogs with me to the kennels, and I could pair them up on dog walks Monday to Friday. But Digger continued to be a difficult dog.

'Why is he doing this?' 'Why is he so naughty' 'Arggghhh!'

This was quite a difference from what I was used to. The guy I was with at the time used disciplinary methods, I knew they didn't work but controlling those emotions became majorly stressful with Digger.

When I walked into the caravan and saw the contents of the walls and floors in tatters, I lost it. *'This dog has got to go!!'*

When you are struggling with your dog, it's hard for your brain to think logically. In place of your thinking brain, comes the emotional one. The ever-increasing thoughts of why this is happening. They should know better by now. What more can I do?

I couldn't fathom why Digger was like this. He was being exercised daily across the fields and paired up with two dogs I was walking at the time in Baslow, so I knew he was getting the exercise. Was it the right type of activity, though?

No, it wasn't. And I was punishing him for being bored. When we use punishment, not only do we compromise the dog's ability to learn, but the lasting effects of it can range from disappointing to disastrous.

You and I both learn best by being taught, practicing what we've been taught, and having constructive criticism or praise when we get things right. Imagine being in front of an audience about to give a presentation you've no knowledge of teaching. You deliver it, and instead of praise and feedback, you get boo-ed and slated for your efforts instead. You leave feeling embarrassed, upset, and your confidence shattered.

Are you going to be in a rush to deliver a presentation like that again?

If your dog does something wrong, wouldn't it be better to show them what to do instead of shouting or punishing them?

Dogs don't speak English. They speak dog. And dogs will chase, chew, jump, eat anything they come across and bite to argue. Remember Jean Donaldson's quote?

Here's another one for you. Although dogs can't speak English, they are masters at reading body language and emotions. When using your tone of voice, your dog won't necessarily understand why you are pissed off with them. They'll just know you're in a foul mood.

Claire Lawrence

And, when using your tone of voice. What behaviours are you actually punishing?

Imagine your dog is:

1. Lunging on the lead/ bouncing at the window
2. Barking
3. Scared

You shout at them to stop the barking and they do. Is this good?

Hold that thought a second. Just because the barking has finished, it doesn't mean this is what you've told them off for. Where's the problem I hear you say.

Which of those three behaviours did you really punish? Since your dog was performing all three of them together, how can you 110% clarify which one it was your dog has been told off for?

If you get a few more yards down the road, or you turn your back in the house to carry on with your jobs and your dog's starts barking again. Trust me when I say, it ain't the barking you've curbed.

'If a man aspires towards a righteous life, his first act of abstinence is from injury to animals" - Albert Einstein.

Solve The Equation

I wasn't a keen academic at school. I'm not now, and one thing I was terrible at was Maths. So much so, I never grasped the whole adding and subtracting thing reliably until my later years on the market. Dishing out the change to buyers soon taught me what to give back to what note or coin. It was more of a learned system than it was working it out.

'You can't walk around with a calculator in your pocket, Claire' said the math teacher to the student. Here, check out my new iPhone, sir... Mwhaha.

I didn't say this. It would have been confiscated. But I thought it!

Reward-based training is just like maths. When you start to break things down and look into it further, the same rules and principals apply. You can add and subtract behaviours. The problem you are facing can be divided into smaller sections, worked on, and multiplied into the desired and finalised sum.

When I get called out to help people with their dogs, the behaviour I am presented with has multiplied out of control. Some saying they've tried reward-based training before, and it hasn't worked for them. Hmmm... me says someone's been doing it wrong.

This style of training is much quicker and more effective than anything else out there. Other than the right process not being followed, another reason people give up with the equation is that their dog reverts to barking again after a certain amount of time.

Claire Lawrence

Undoing a previously learned behaviour like barking takes time. Your dog knows it works, so teaching them to stay quiet will take longer. Your dog will also go through a testing phase where they revisit the barking and give it another shot. This is the stage where people think things aren't working.

Or there's another one... let me compose myself for a second. *Big intake of breath*
People thinking using rewards is only bribery.

It isn't, but I can see how this may be interpreted. To the human and untrained eye, throwing food and toys around for dogs doesn't look that effective. Especially when they stop finding the food and then bark, but it isn't the food at fault.

Food is THE quickest route into sorting out your training and behaviour problems, and it doesn't and shouldn't result in fat dogs. All four of my dogs are treat trained, they get their breakfast portion biscuit by biscuit from my training pouch.

This is a trick you are likely missing out on. Let's say for argument's sake there are 100 biscuits in your dog's dinner bowl, twice a day. You are wasting 200 opportunities to train your dog and teach them a new skill. Your dog will much prefer working this way, and I have client's dog's now who won't eat from the food bowl. They wait until they can work for it.

200 biscuits do sound a lot. Though it's what your dog would be eating anyway, so why aren't you using it. You could quite quickly start by rewarding your dog for being calm and quiet. Well, it's where I would begin anyway, but

I'll come onto the photograph training in *'Figure It Out Fast'* Chapter.

Using food in this way not only allows you to train your dog, get their eyes on you but you can and will begin to re-wire the brain. Literally!

With Titon, although it took longer than it should have done. What with doing everything wrong. We did get there eventually. With all of the work, I had put into preventing him from barking and supporting him whenever he felt scared. When the time came for me to move to a new house, into a busier and more distracting environment. I was unsure.

I no longer had the use of those open fields and escape routes. Unless I popped him in the car, but I knew I couldn't avoid distractions forever.

By dividing his barking problem into tiny fragments and adding rewards whenever those good behaviours were present. It definitely helped with the move. I can't recall our first walk in the village precisely but what I can remember is it was a long one.

From my house, when you take a left, you head right into the thick of it. It's a quiet village, but the fruit and veg shop, the butchers and the post office are the in places to go around here. What I do remember is hooking up Titon, Skye, and Digger on the leads and just going for it.

Another two dogs in the picture I hear you say. Yeah, things had got to the point where Titon was accepting of other household dogs. The first to integrate was Skye, and I was so nervous about this. She was tiny, and up against a dog so large, I was on high alert when we did it, but it worked, and they became the best of friends.

Digger's introduction didn't go so smoothly. Mainly because he's a live wire and Titon was a dog who wasn't to be disturbed much. Although they weren't the perfect match and we did have a couple of fights between them, it was always Digger who started the problem.

Anyway, off we went. Dogs in tow down the village high-street. We passed the local drinking establishment, past the butchers. People waiting at the bus stop, no problem. Then past the last pub and we were out of the village. It took us five minutes; the village is so small.

As we continued walking down the pavement towards Tideswell dale, I didn't really know what to expect. It was our first proper walk, and I had no clue what was there. How busy it would be. How many off-lead dogs would be around. It was like walking blind.

All turned out fine, and the only distractions we encountered were off lead cows and a couple of dogs. Both Shepherds showing little interest. Digger doing his frustrated bouncy and crying dance.

This prevention and capturing phase I had been doing with Titon before coming to the village, had worked. Even with the higher levels of emotions in digger, I think Titon did one short sharp woof, but it wasn't to the distractions. If he were talking English, he would have been saying 'Pack it in Digs!'

Divide up the problem, subtract the chances and places for your dog to bark in.

To Neuter Or Not To Neuter, This Is The Question.

When Titon began to display unwanted barking behaviour. One of the first things I was told to do and believed would help was to neuter him. This is a widespread thought process in barking dogs to resolve the issue. I fell for it!

It's not hard to see why people think this way. It almost feels like the common sense thing to do, doesn't it? The reason for this is because people tend to associate testosterone with an increase in aggression. Especially in male dogs. So naturally, removing the source and having less testosterone, in theory, should equal a calmer and more docile dog, right?

Another major factor behind people thinking this way is, unfortunately, there is still a lot of dog behaviour advice in the media culture. It tends to pin most canine-related issues on dominance or conflicts over social status.

One of the first things I did when Titon barked was research. Shit research I may add but research all the same. I decided to proceed and take him to be castrated because this is what everything was telling me to do. Boy, what a big mistake I made.

Two things happened after 'the snip.' Not only did his barking increase, but he also then hated the vet's. Upon removal of said dangly bits, his fear increased. I had effectively removed any remaining bits of confidence in him by removing the testosterone. And whatever happened in the vet's surgery I'll never know.

I still laugh about this day, and I'm giggling right now, just writing this out. I remember entering the surgery and being told where Titon was. I thought this strange and presumed they'd bring him out to me. On the way through to the pens, the vet said to me everything had gone to plan, but they'd had issues in checking him over.

I looked through the glass tops in the door, and there was my boy lying down looking, to the left of him. His eyes fixed on something. Another dog, I thought. It wasn't until another vet came past his kennel when he tried to lunge and get at them, though not being able to give a full extent of the lunge from his down.

'We haven't been allowed in the kennel, he might be okay with you, but be careful' said the vet.

As I entered through the doors, and he glanced up towards where I was, the vets were amazed. He was up wagging his tail, crying at the gate and I just went straight in.

'Well, it's like a temperament transplant'

I heard from behind me as I was having greeting cuddles with my boy. Being handed a lead and bringing him out of the kennel, I had no issues at all. Although Titon couldn't resist having just one more *'Fuck off'* woof and made a mini lunge towards the closest vet.

I couldn't blame him at all as he jumped out of the way and returned to whatever he wasn't doing at the other side of the kennel area.

After recovery, this barking was still happening. It hadn't helped at all. So, I was still experiencing lunging, barking, and snapping. There's no going back once the deed has been done. Unless you wanna attach Christmas baubles there, but it won't bring back the testosterone.

What happened here is although testosterone can act as a confidence booster, in some cases, the absence of it, after castration can mean your dog becomes more delicate and less confident emotionally. The same happened with Digger, but I did this with him because he squirted pee everywhere where he walked. In the house in plain sight of me, daily.

Castrating and spaying for females is not a quick fix to eliminating a barking dog. Hunter, my youngest is still, as we call, entire. He's got the full works, and I'm in no hurry to whip em off. He's not the most confident of dogs and although we encounter the testosterone time of the month, where he pesters the feck out of the other dogs, I'd rather this than reducing his confidence.

I understand why both vets and rescue workers insist on castration, but this is to reduce medical and breeding problems. Behaviourally, undergoing this operation either too early or for the wrong circumstances, is actually increasing fearful responses in dogs.

With the way the dog population is today, and there being so many out of control dogs around doing whatever the hell they want. It's logical to prevent problems like this. It wouldn't be long before the dog park became the creation of a whole mixture of breeds.

A labrashitzu anyone?
What about a Bermesapoo?
Heck, let's get a threesome in there and go for a Jack-Bull-Shitz.

My imagination ran away with me there, but you get the point.

To finish this section, if you're thinking about neutering to cure your barking dog, then please reconsider it. There is a high probability it isn't going to rectify the problem.

The smart dog owners first find out Why their dog is barking, before making any rushed decisions. And if you've already done the deed, then yeah sure there ain't any going back on it. You just have to keep working to build your dog's confidence and doing so in a planned and strategic way which will help and support them

I'll come on to this shortly.

Chapter Five: Figure It Out Fast! You 3 Steps To Silence

Your 3 steps to silence training now begins. Although you have already received a goldmine full of information, which I wanna recap to make sure you're on the … same page.

First up is taking your dogs to the vets. Don't even think about skipping out on this part. It's more important than anything. No amount of training will fix a poorly or in pain pooch.

Then you are to sit with a pen and paper for a few minutes each time, in different locations. Just watching and taking notes on your dog's behaviour.

Next up is the video recording to find out why your dog is barking. If you find your dog's body language doesn't correlate with the 'Fear Barkers Body Guide,' then they could be barking for another reason. Either way, please get a professional to help you with this properly.

Remember you can get access to the relaxed and fearful body language diagrams online, by heading to this website: www.3sts.co.uk/

You have learned what to watch out for in your dog's body language via the HELPS guide. It's essential to look at the whole picture of your dog, but as a guideline, these are things to watch out for in terms of doggy unhappiness.

We've spoken about a lot so far, and I recommend you read this book more than once. It's also useful to revert back to if you are unsure of something, so please use the resources available to you and let's get cracking with getting you a quieter and calmer, canine companion.

Intellectuals Solve Problems, Genius' Prevent Them!

When I tell people to prevent the barking from occurring, I'm met with confusion and doubt.

'What's that gonna teach them?'
'How am I supposed to stop them barking?'
'It's impossible, I'm surrounded by distractions all of the time.'

I used to love going on adventures with Titon, and I loved it even more when people stopped me when he was a puppy in Nottingham to admire and meet him. On our treks, we could end up anywhere. Along the wild jagged rocks on the cliff tops. Exploring the abandoned buildings in the fields.

Sitting by the tent next to the hilltops. Streams as clear as air and just watch the wildlife world go by. When I moved to Buxton, I just used to leave the caravan door open, and he'd go in and out as he pleased.

When his behaviour changed, so did our walks. There were no more clifftop walks or leaving the caravan door open anymore. I had to keep him on the lead and secured. All I had left were the open fields.

Which served us well. I never particularly enjoyed congregating with other people on the dog walks anyway. I still don't to this day. I'm quite the lone wolf, and with-it content. As I've mentioned before, distance is essential. The further away the perceived threat is, the less likely your dog will bark.

You and I both know it isn't going to solve the barking problem completely, but less barking and more teaching of other, good behaviours. Will prevent it from getting any worse before you can move onto the next stages.

Here's another thing I'll tell you about a barking dog. They don't need to go for a walk every single day. For the fearful dog, being put into the same scary situations daily is gonna keep adding to their stress levels. I regularly take days off from walking my own dogs. It's a given for the boys, especially if they have barked on a walk.

Don't get me wrong, I get how physical exercise is beneficial. But just like you and me we can put on or lose weight whenever we want. The mental state of your dog is more important, in my opinion. Living in a constant state of fear isn't good for anybody.

As a youngster with Titon, I did this inadvertently actually. Some days, I'd just let him out to the toilet in the morning and then slob out in front of the TV for the rest of the day. I didn't realise at the time how useful this was in his routine.

It's something I'm much more aware of and schedule in each week for the boys. At one time Hunter was so struck with stress, panic, and fear we couldn't get out of the front door without him barking and panicking. Kicked up a real fuss he did whether something was there or not.

Hunter was grabbed at around 8-10 months of age and pinned to the floor by his nose. There were no physical injuries obtained, but it was enough for him to learn other dogs were scary. So, instead of forcing him to go outside into the big bad world, I gave him ten days off.

Yeah, that's right, I didn't walk him for almost two weeks, and he fucking loved it. Compared to Skye, he's a lazy GSD, but he is mentally active. In giving your dog a day off, don't go thinking you can get away without doing anything. You do have to tire their mind; this is easy to do when you know-how.

If you do this correctly, you won't get a bored dog, and you won't come home to a terrier's millionaire wallpaper lifestyle.

Prevention is the opposite of what most people will do. Remember me taking Titon down to the Pavilion Gardens to 'get him used to it?' It's like running backward on a running machine. It won't get you anywhere.

I have listed some of the most common preventative measures you can take and use straight away with your dog.

- Avoid busy areas. Stay in your garden or pop your dog in the car. Go somewhere quiet. Whether it's dogs, people, traffic, or pink elephants. Just avoid them. Turning around on a walk is okay to do. Even if you borrow someone's driveway for a minute or two.
- If they bark out of the window, then close your curtains and leave the TV or music on in the background.

- Barks at the postman? As above, but you can also attach a post box outside of the house. Dogs know the sound of the letterbox.

When putting it this way, it sounds so simple, doesn't it? Common sense almost. And it is. Dog training does not have to be complicated.

Here's one for you. I have four working breeds of dogs, and they have approximately 15-20 minutes' worth of exercise, between them all, twice a day. For only four days of the week. One day of the week, they will get a session outside and off the lead. Separately and in a quiet location. We may not walk more than 100 yards, instead opting for playing together and training. The other two days they don't leave the house at all other than to toilet in the back yard.

How can I possibly keep my dogs from not tearing the house to pieces with such little exercise? Well, it's because I tire their brains. I don't do daily hikes, I certainly won't be found throwing tennis balls around constantly for them and truth be told, the last thing I want to do after being out training and walking all day, is another two, one-hour walks.

The days vary on when we go out. I like Sunday mornings and early when everyone is recovering from Saturday night hangovers, and the village has fewer tourists floating around. They can get cut short sometimes, especially with Digger. I don't care much for dealing with removing his jaws from another dog when it's easier for me to turn around and go somewhere else. Or home.

Intellects solve problems, geniuses prevent them.

Take a day off with your dog. The more days off in the initial stages of training you can do, the better. I'm talking like a week here. Don't keep putting them in a situation where they will bark. Sure, sometimes it can't be helped, and some fucker will knacker things up for you. Ahem...

But the less your dog barks, the more their stress levels decrease. Think about how relaxing it is when you go on holiday. No worries, no daily chores to worry about. It's feet up and forget everything else. This is how your dog will start to feel.

And don't forget to tire their minds too. Otherwise, you will have a boredom problem.

ADORE

'We got separated from each other because of some "misunderstanding," I loved you, and you loved me, but then we parted ways. Destiny was very nice to me it gave you back to me, and I was happy.' - Dharam Singh Rathore

What does your dog love? I mean really love, not just something they'll take for the sake of it. For some dogs, food is god. Others go crazy coo-koo for their favourite toy. Some dogs just love being with their owners.

Whichever it is, there is an element I've picked up on briefly at the beginning of this book but not something I've gone into greater detail on, until now. Something you must have between you and your dog, and it's something you don't need to forget.

It's the thing you always have with you, all the time.

Skye, my eldest German Shepherd, naturally wants to herd and chase things. Everything she is genetically designed to do. Though she's my oracle of goodness anyway and has a tip-top recall.

I once kept pigs. My old spot was bred with pure Wild Boar, and this produces a breed called Iron Age. These twelve piglets were definitely, genetically more wild boar than they were domesticated. Gordon Bennet's they didn't half cause me some bloody problems.

For about three weeks, these little sods kept getting out of the enclosed and wired pigpen. How they did it will be an eye-opener on intelligence for you but let me get on with my original story of what you always need to have with your dog and the things you've always got with you.

On this occasion back up the field in my truck, Skye in the back with the pig pellets and me armed with my horse bucket for re-capturing I found them not too far from the pen entrance. When they saw me arrive, they came flying over to me wanting food. Not like they were starving either, they got fed twice a day and more when I had to coax them back in the pen time after time.

I remember this incident well. There's a phrase almost every pig farmer will know and one that's always to be followed. Never fall down in a pigpen.

118

My Old Spot was bang on, a little like a dog really. She loved her belly scratches and trusted me without a doubt. She allowed me in with her piglets from day one. It's a good job she did really because it wasn't until I was almost on top of her within the pen, I realised the dangers of what I'd done. And the exit would have been too far to outrun her if she took a dislike to me being there. I'd have been fucked!

These piglets grow, and I had no attachment or trust with these the same way as I did my pig. They were young, wild, and more often than not, free. It took the phrase Free-Range Pigs to another level.

I've also seen what a Wild Boar can do. A feral pig who are omnivorous, meaning they eat both plants and meat. They would kill one of their own and can never be fully domesticated.

I grabbed me bucket from the truck and started to scatter the pellets into it, headed over to the pen entrance and then heard the almighty squawking and squealing a troop of pigs make. As I turned around, I see Skye somewhat attempting to herd them. Me realising she'd not been told to stay. *'Whoops!'*

Okay, so now I had a German Shepherd loose with no idea what she'd just thrown herself in the middle of and a group of bloodthirsty piglets not at all happy with her presence. Fuck.

I panicked when I saw the male boars in the group turn their intentions towards the four-legged foreigner in their 'troop' and initiated a charge. I was and still am, grateful she listens to me intently and has been well trained. This is where the secret weapon came into play. The one you will never be without.

Trust.

During the panic-ridden frenzy of squealing pigs, a worried dog owner and Skye realising she was about to shit a brick. I needed her to listen to me.

'Skye away!' I shouted, and she ran. She took off up the field racing along the wall side, stopping every so often to look back at me. The whole troop of pigs now in full pursuit of her.

'AWAY, GO ON, GO!!' Off she went.

As she reached the top end of the field, she performed a half-circle circuit back toward where the truck was stationed. My facial muscles contracted involuntarily, and I started to cringe. This corner cur was a little too close for comfort, and those pigs were gaining speed.

Skye was high on the pig feeding frenzy list now. She was being hunted. I shouted her name at the top of my voice in sheer and utter panic. *'SKYE'* I indicated a hand signal *'LEFT, GO LEFT!'*

As she turned and narrowly avoided her back end being flung up by the leading pig, I whistled her which means get your ass back here now! Well, it means to come here, but those were the words I was muttering under my breath on this day.

Racing at full speed back towards me, she had gained some distance and reached the pick up safely. The pigs weren't too far behind her, but I had enough time to get her in the back and shut the door. As I heard the catch connect and Skye safe from the chase. I momentarily froze as I realised, I was now the only target available.

'Erm. Holy shit' With two bust knees and the pigs virtually at my feet, what the hell do I do now? Am I a sitting duck or do I run? I can tell you now there was no way I'd have made it into the safety of the vehicle. No way. The trust element helped to get Skye out of danger, but as I stated before, no way in hell or high water, I trusted these piglets.

So, I did what any ... I suppose I can't say normal because it wasn't normal. I stood and shook my bucket. We must have had some sort of connection because this saved my ass. I was clearly still viewed as a resource to this troop, and they're a highly intelligent species. Whether it would pull them out of the hunting mode, I had no clue at the time. But it did, and I lived to tell this curly wurly piglet tail.

Trust is an element you cannot afford to lose with your dog, and do you know what. It's dead simple to do when you know-how. Here, let me guide you through it. Build the trust, build the bond, and I'm trying to think of some James Bond caption to finish this sentence off in style. But I can't, so let's move on.

ADORE

Remembering the dog has two brain settings. Thinking and emotional. You may read through this and say my dog won't eat or play with me while outside. I can't get his attention, or he just isn't listening. Well, they'll be a reason for this, which is why I recommend you start this training in a setting your dog is comfortable in.

Animate
Distract
Operate
Reward
Entertain

Animate: Dogs love to chase and find things. Do you know how easy it can be to regain a dog's focus if you use a 'chase me' game or provide something for them to sniff out? Really easy, under the right circumstances. Please don't chase your dog, you're just gonna create a recall problem. They quickly find the solution is running off from you. Be it through play or shock of being chased.

I find the easiest way to recreate things your dog loves is to lose those inhibitions. Roll a treat along the floor for them to 'chase and consume.' If you've got a longer lead or they're off it, run away from them while calling their name. Or you can use toys, preferable two of the same toys and play tug or mini fetch.

I say mini fetch because I'm not a fan of excessive tennis ball chasing. I do use tennis balls, but it's mainly to give my dog something else to chase when we are passing livestock gates, and the cows or sheep are close enough for my dogs to notice and go to investigate them.

Get creative here and find out what it is, your dog loves to interact with. I'm talking all eyes on you when you have this item in your possession.

I have a varying degree of rewards for my guys. The tennis ball is the ultimate prize, and this is used in more distracting environments or in the use of an emergency. I can see their eyes light up when I remove a ball from my pocket. Even more so, for a squeaky one.

I use their breakfast in the morning or during the walks in the day. They are still being fed, just not from their bowl. Sniffing for the food is my preferred choice, but we also do catch it, chase the biscuit and rewarding for any good behaviour. Which I'll come onto more in the next step to silence success.

Distract : I get a little taken a back with the words just distract them or bribery. To some degree, we are diverting our dogs from the things we don't want them to bark at. Though it isn't just a case of distraction. When we provide fun, support, and rewards, we are effectively rewiring their brain.

'I see something I'm scared of. Mum tells me everything is okay and I get some cooked chicken to find on the floor. Meh, okay it isn't so scary anymore.'

This is an example of how dogs learn. If we are pairing something really valuable, with something scary. Providing the distance is large enough. Soon your dog will learn, when they see a dog, it's been ingrained into them to lower their head to the floor and sniff. Make sure you always reward this action. This is something we definitely want to see more of.

This distraction of food or a game of tug, for example, isn't just a distraction but keep 'distracting' your dog. The more you do, the less the bark. The more they learn what to do instead. Providing you are consistent and have things set up correctly, you will quickly see your dog learn to control their emotions and perform the manoeuvre automatically. Always reward this!

Overemphasis: When your dog does something right, how do you show them they've done an excellent job. Is it a quick *'good boy'* or does it get ignored? Overemphasising the success your dog has performed is beneficial to you both.

Not only will it show your dog you are happy with the decision they have made, but you also approve of it. It also makes you feel better, as well. Too often, as barking dog owners, we face negativity. Disappointed, embarrassment, and judgement. Your dog experiencing fear, stress, and being told off.

Happiness is a broad term that describes the experience of positive emotions. Research shows being happier doesn't just make you feel better; it also brings a host of potential health benefits. Being happy promotes a range of lifestyle habits, important to our overall health.

Regular physical activity helps to build strong bones, increase energy levels, decrease body fat, and lowers blood pressure. It can help improve sleeping habits, which is vital for concentration, productivity, and appears to boost the immune system.

Being happy helps to combat stress. Stress you and I both feel when out walking with our barking dogs.

So, when your dog does something right, overemphasis just how well they've done. It builds your confidence and theirs. Plus, if the behaviour has been adequately rewarded, the likelihood of it being repeated, will increase.

Reward: We've spoken about finding out what it is, your dog adores. All you need to do now is keep using it. I tend to have a structure for what and how I reward. In keeping with the Animation section, I use a technique called the Pendulum.

This is simply a left to right, or forward and backward motion of rewarding. I literally throw a treat in front of me, then the next one goes behind me. I reward often, especially in the early stages of training. The beauty of the Pendulum is it's predictable. Your dog soon catches on to the routine.

This is fantastic not only for focusing your dog but also loose lead walking, stops to heel, and the most important one. FUN! I always give a *'Yay'* or *'Good Boy'* when the dog I have gets hold of the reward. This is an easier technique to do with food, but it can be done with toys too. Check out the resources section on the website if you wanna see it in action.

www.3sts.co.uk/

Rewards equal results.

Entertain: It sounds so simple and ties in with everything you've learned in ADORE so far. Animating the chase is fun. Distracting your dog rewires their brain. Overemphasising their success is beneficial for you both in terms of happiness. Rewarding frequently and in a pendulum, motion improves basic obedience and behaviour. Entertaining your dog is the whole concept of how I teach.

If you're out with them and have your head stuck in your phone. Aren't in the moment with your dog on the walk or aren't taking into consideration what your dog is learning out there every day. Then things won't go well for you.

I was on a training session with Charlie a Bernese Mountain dog last week. She used to drag her owners everywhere and had a problem controlling her excited emotions. A big dog who put me through my paces when she wanted to go.

Anyway, as we were plodding along, I looked up to see a man with his spaniel approaching. I instantly recognised the dog and then realised I had done a one to one session him previously. His dog was rescued and was continually pulling on the lead. The owner also had an issue getting and keeping her attention.

One of the main things he took away from our session was playing together. I regularly saw Lucy, the spaniel, and her owner on the common in Buxton. Him engaging in play, her off the lead and 110% focused on him. He listened, he found out exactly what Lucy loved. He practiced it and now has a dog who doesn't pull on the lead and wants to be with him.

Can Everyone Please Just Chill Out!

Settling inside of the house is normally much easier for your dog than it is outside. Well, for some dogs anyway.

We went through a phase of the dogs not settling properly in the house because they were always on edge. Someone I lived with had a temperament which was up and down like a prostitute's knickers, even I didn't know whether he'd be in a good mood or a bad. Which affected the dog's as he came home or downstairs.

I imagine, at the moment. Your dog views the walk or some form of attachment to the barking as being stressful. I get this is hard for all involved, remember my Hunter story? We couldn't get out of the door without him panicking and barking, and he certainly wasn't settled.

However, if you follow the steps, I have suggested so far, plus so more of this activity too. Then we can soon increase the settled state of mind and body within your dog, whether inside or out. It's all about making things pleasant for your dog.

Okay, hold onto your seats because this is one of my favourite things to teach. The reason I like it so much is not only because I prefer calm over chaos, but I love seeing the dogs be able to switch off and chill, even on something as distracting as a walk. Smells, sights, emotions, and more to contend with. If your dog can settle down outside, this is an excellent skill for them.

I do this on every single walk and session.

The settle:

It's worthwhile teaching your dog a walk isn't all go, go, go. Either through excitement or nerves to get the fuck home. What I will say here is to start this in a super successful location. You will likely fail if you try to do this when there are things around to take your dog's attention from you. I like to do this about half way through our walks, though I always mix it up and never do it in the same location every time.

From my perspective, if I ever want to stop and grab a coffee, or more likely a beer on walks with my guys, I'd like to know that with the right location and distance, my dogs can chill out too.

Before we begin, I wouldn't recommend using a toy for this activity. Toys are too exciting, and you'll probably find your dog won't be able to stay still. Though for some dogs, food can be too exciting too, so you can always use the TOUCH points training to relax and use bog-standard, less exciting food to help with this.

Another thing I recommend, we'll get started soon promise! Is teaching this behaviour on some portable bedding such as vet bedding or a thing mat. Make sure it's easy to carry... I have seen people bring full-on bedding into my classrooms before now, and it isn't a practical item to take on a walk. By doing this, your dog will associate the mat with the behaviour required.

Right let's go! To ensure success, we are going to start this in the house or the area your dog is most settled already. No distractions, okay.

Settle is effectively a lie-down. However, it's slightly different from a down because your dog can pick their own way of relaxing in position. Ideally, we want a relaxed down where the hips are to one side, opposed to a dog on his back with legs in the air, but whatever works for your pooch.

Settle is an emotional state of mind, as much as it is a physical behaviour. This is more about your dog switching off to training and not staying alert for the next thing you ask of them. You can help your dog to success by practicing this at a time where they are already tired. After your ADORE game, each day would be perfect.

Pick a comfortable place to start the exercise. If your dog already knows how to lie down, then simply ask them too. On the mat. If they can't lie down, let's teach them!

Start with your dog in a sit. A behaviour most dogs do well. Take a small treat and imagine gluing it to their nose. Slowly, I want you to start lowering your hand with the treat in, down towards the floor, in a straight line. Don't go luring them across the room, otherwise, they'll get up.

When on the floor, give them the treat. You may need to repeat this a few times. Some dogs get up before you've reached the floor, which is cool we just need to practice. Other dogs will happily hunch over and just slump into a down. Once this happens, it's time to get them to stay there.

I do this by placing the treats on the floor and in between the paws. On the floor is important okay, don't be tempted to feed them to the mouth. While ever your dog stays in position, keep firing those treats down in a steady stream. Like you're firing a rifle bullet after bullet.

You need to learn to avoid eye contact with your dog as much as possible. Unlike most of the things I have taught you so far, this is the one exercise where we want to be less interesting.

The rules of this 'game' are simple. If your dog is lying down, they get fed. If they get up, feeding stops until they are lying down again. If they get up, don't worry, just re-peat the process again. Over time and with daily practice, we can start to progress the behaviour more and more, which means using fewer treats.

If you're more of a visual learner, then head to the website www.3sts.co.uk/settle to see the training in action.

Couple of things to remember. If you put your hand in your pocket to get a treat, your dog will expect you to deliver. At this stage just keep a handful of treats in your hand to feed them with. I progress this behaviour in my barking dog online course where you get more reliability and longer duration.

Now, you can use a word if you want too, but as with anything, I like people to stay quiet. When it boils down to it, and if you are training on a mat. The sight of the mat or a point to the floor will be enough. But if you really wanna use a word, then I use settle.

Once you've nailed this inside, then you can take it outside and practice in quiet locations.

Small Steps = Success

Bloody hell, where did the time go! I can't believe this is the final section of the book. I hope you've enjoyed reading it because I've certainly enjoyed sharing all of this with you. There are many valuable treasures in here which will get you silence success.

Remember though, everything starts with you. If you don't put in the effort, you can kiss goodbye to the magic of a muted mutt. So, make sure you practice daily.

You now have a solid plan of action, which I will recap for you shortly, so it's all in one place to refer back too. I want to first take this time to thank the people in my life who made this whole thing possible. Without them, you wouldn't be reading this book.

All of the confidence I had when growing up got taken away from me, and I never fully appreciated just how capable I was of completing things I wanted to do. But also doing things I never thought I possibly could. Some people who said they were proud of me, deep down made a lot of attempts to prevent me from moving forward. Intentionally too.

It wasn't until October 2018 when I watched a video from my business mentor, which really made me 'man up' and get rid of the problems I was facing. I had adapted to the nonsense and lived day in, day out the same way. After getting rid of the things holding me back, I have had much more success with everything. More so, my own barking dogs and their training.

Yes, my boys still bark, but in comparison to where they were, it's improved dramatically. I'm living proof that when you set your mind to doing something, staying consistent with it, and putting in the work. Even on those days, you can't be arsed too, things do pay off in the end.

Sure, I fuck up sometimes. But who doesn't? What I'm really saying with all of this is, it's okay to be yourself, and it's okay to make mistakes. It's how we learn, and it's how you come back from and rectify them, that truly counts.

Don't be afraid to stand up for your dog and the things you believe in.
Don't give up at the first hurdle because shit went wrong.
Don't be a sheep in the herd, following the wrong advice and heading in the wrong direction.

So, without further ado, I send my greatest thanks to all of the following people.

To Dominic Hodgson, the Petbizwiz. Not only for pushing me to write this book but for everything else in between. You've helped me to grow both the business and in myself. Without you, I really would be stuck in the same monotonous routine and a feeling of never getting anywhere or being as productive, as I am today.

To my mother, Debbie Lawrence. The support and help you've provided over all these years with the backing of whatever I do in my life, but also at those times when things went wrong between us. I am eternally grateful to have someone as supportive and as encouraging as you in my life. Plus, we make pretty good drinking buddies too.

To every pet professional who assisted in the draft reading of this book and offering of support through any of those shitty times. You know who you are, and I am so lucky to have found you all. Keep kicking ass mofos.

To all of my clients, I cannot explain how lucky I am to have you on my team. I love working with you, and I love seeing your dog's progress. Growing into confident, calm, and happy canines.

Here's to a future of exactly that my friend.

Adios amigo,
Claire.

The Lessons Learnt

Prevention: How more distance away from the scary thing, is always the best option to take. Especially in the early stages of rehabilitation. Take a day a week at least and ensure you are always tiring your dog's mind.

TOUCH: Testing which areas your dog likes to be touched, can be useful to use when they get panicked or unsure. My preferences are on the front chest, and the hind legs. But test where your dog likes first. Then use it to support them and build confidence.

HELPS: Hackles. Ears. Low Posture. Posture. Sound of the bark.

SETTLE: Teaching your dog to relax on cue is worth its weight in gold. Use a mat, practice this daily after your walks or training sessions.

CHARM TO CALM: Turn the shouting into silence, by staying calm. Try not to bother your dog too much, other than offering support when it's needed.

CAPTURING: Remember to keep taking imaginary photos of your dog's good behaviours. When you see them perform the good, reward them!

Always see things from your dog's perspective. This is the only perspective to truly matter.

Always choose a reputable pet professional and ensure you have taken your dog to the vets for a full medical check-up. You must rule out medical causes BEFORE starting the training to stop them barking.

Record your dog's barking and tally it against the Fear Barkers Body Guide. It is also worth getting a professional assessment too.

Use Maths To Solve Your Training Problems: Divide up the problem into segments. Take away the cause of the barking. Add more rewards and things your dog enjoys doing. Then watch the good stuff multiply.

"You cannot expect your dog's behaviour to change, unless you first start to change your own"- Claire Lawrence, 'The Dog Charmer' 2019

48455275R00080

Printed in Poland
by Amazon Fulfillment
Poland Sp. z o.o., Wrocław